Sports Illustrated

BASKETBALL
The Keys to Excellence

Sports Illustrated Winner's Circle Books

BOOKS ON TEAM SPORTS

Baseball
Basketball
Football: Winning Defense
Football: Winning Offense
Hockey
Lacrosse
Pitching
Soccer

BOOKS ON INDIVIDUAL SPORTS

Bowling
Competitive Swimming
Cross-Country Skiing
Figure Skating
Golf
Racquetball
Running for Women
Skiing
Tennis
Track: Championship Running
Track: The Field Events

SPECIAL BOOKS

Backpacking
Canoeing
Fly Fishing
Scuba Diving
Small-Boat Sailing
Strength Training

Sports Illustrated

BASKETBALL
The Keys to Excellence

by Neil D. Isaacs and Dick Motta

Sports Illustrated
Winner's Circle Books
New York

Picture credits: Basketball Hall of Fame, p. 11; Rich Clarkson, 8, 22, 34; John Iacono, 15 (bottom), 31; Richard Mackson, 24, 95, 106; Manny Millan, 15, 28, 54, 67, 69, 70; Peter Read Miller, 3, 25, 37, 56, 78; Carl Skalak, Jr., 33; George Tiedemann, 59; Tony Triolo, 58; David E. Klutho, 42 (top); Scott Cunningham, 42 (bottom); John Biever, 43; Jerry Wachter, 46, 48; John W. McDonough, 64. All other photographs by Walter Iooss, Jr.

Library of Congress Cataloging-in-Publication Data

Isaacs, Neil David, 1931–
    Sports illustrated basketball : the keys to excellence / by Neil
D. Isaacs and Dick Motta ; photography by Walter Iooss, Jr.
      p.   cm. — (Sports illustrated winner's circle books)
    ISBN 0-452-26207-0
    1. Basketball. I. Motta, Dick. II. Sports illustrated (Time,
inc.) III. Title. IV. Title: Basketball. V. Series.
GV885.I73 1988
796.32′32—dc19
                                                   88-18595
90 91 92 AG/HL 10 9 8 7 6 5 4 3

Contents

BASKETBALL

The Keys to Excellence

Introduction to Basketball

We have all heard the stories of how young Bill Bradley or young Isiah Thomas or young Larry Bird spent hour after hour in all kinds of weather, alone, throwing a ball in a hoop. But the truth is that those stories are not all that exceptional. Because basketball, unlike any other team sport, allows a player to practice the simple skills—his moves, his shots—by himself and at great length. And he can enjoy doing it.

Basketball begins and ends by being fun. Even in solitary practice there is the challenge of hitting a target. With just one friend there can be a game, one on one, or at least companionship and competition in the practice of skills. Any number can play, up to the full complement of ten, and basketball is just as satisfying, half court as much as full court, pavement as much as hardwood or Tartan, a schoolyard or driveway as much as the Forum or the Spectrum or Madison Square Garden.

The invention and spread of basketball is a story of fortunate circumstances and coincidences. The Young Men's Christian Association school in Springfield, Massachusetts, was a training school for athletic directors and YMCA secretaries. Its graduates went to posts all over the country, taking their Springfield routines with

College basketball at its exciting best—a slam dunk in the N.C.A.A. championships.

them, and they also often returned to the school like former seminarians seeking guidance from the seat of their order. Besides, they all kept abreast of what was going on at Springfield through *The Triangle,* their monthly newsletter.

James Naismith, who had come from Bennie's Corners in northern Ontario to study for the ministry at McGill University, decided that there was great potential for spiritual leadership in athletics and enrolled at the Springfield school in 1890 under Dr. Luther Gulick. Naismith stayed on as instructor the following year and was given two difficult assignments by Dean Gulick. One was to devise an indoor activity to sustain athletic interest during the long New England months between the football and baseball seasons. The other was to restore order in a gymnastics class of very competitive and bored young men. Naismith solved both problems with the invention of basketball.

Naismith looked to football, rugby, soccer, water polo, field hockey, and his favorite, lacrosse, for inspiration, but he substantially created the game by a rational process of itemizing his requirements and finding answers to those needs. Naismith's basic perception was that athletic interest could not be sustained in a gym class without a ball in a game, and he had tinkered with the idea of throwing a ball into a receptacle target even before leaving Montreal. It followed, then, since the idea was to play indoors, that the ball should be large and light. The ball should be handled with the hands without a bat, stick, or racquet, but to prevent roughness there would be no running with the ball. Both teams would occupy the same area and no player would be restricted from getting the ball, but there was to be no contact. The ball would be put into play with a center jump as in water polo or rugby, but with only one player from each side. Finally came the crucial and distinctive feature that improved on all ball-goal games: The goal would be elevated and horizontal.

With these principles in mind, Naismith drew up the original thirteen rules and posted them for the class. Mr. Stebbins, the custodian, was asked to supply boxes for the goals, but he had none of suitable size and suggested two peach baskets. These were fastened, at about ten feet high, from the track balcony that circled the gym, and the first game was played on Monday, December 21, 1891, with the eighteen-man class divided into teams of nine.

Success was instantaneous. Frank Mahan, one of the leaders of the class, suggested "Naismith Ball" as the name of the new sport, but when the inventor demurred, Mahan offered the alternative "basket ball." Within a couple of weeks, starting during the Christmas vacation, the game was introduced in several hometowns by members of Naismith's class.

Within a few years basketball had caught on in many places throughout the country, largely under the auspices of the YMCA and through the game's

James Naismath, creator of the game of basketball.

immediate appeal to spectators, until by the turn of the century the colleges had begun to dominate the game for both men and women.

The rules have evolved in a complex and dynamic way over the years, but Naismith's principles have continued to guide. In another irony, there have been many attempts to curb the advantages of height, but each anti-tall rule has forced big men to learn the full range of basketball skills. There remain some rules discrepancies, particularly in the varied use of a time clock for forcing teams to shoot, but basketball continues to develop toward uniformity.

American teams played exhibitions at the 1904 Olympics and again in 1924 and 1928. Finally at the Olympics in Berlin in 1936, after a vigorous campaign led by Kansas Coach Phog Allen, basketball became an official event with twenty-two countries entered. Now, well over a hundred nations are represented in the international basketball federation (FIBA), while professional basketball flourishes on four continents. Basketball is America's gift to the world of team sports, but the game has not yet peaked. Organized basketball is played in ninety-nine percent of all institutions of higher education in the United States, and women's basketball continues to grow steadily.

Many developments in basketball and in media coverage have brought the sport into great prominence as a spectacle. NBA playoffs, Olympic championships, and NCAA tournaments are highlights of any sports fan's calendar and television programming. State high school tourneys are also major gate attractions along with all-star games at every level. And the superstars of the game are often regarded as supreme among our athletes. But what is most impressive about basketball is not the success of its showcase performances but the fact that more people everywhere, at every level, continue to play the game.

1

Fundamentals: Skills and Drills

One of the beautiful things about basketball is the way it makes use of the basic athletic skills: running, jumping, handling a ball, bouncing it, passing it, catching it, and throwing it to a target. In this section let's look at the nature and function of the basketball fundamentals and see how each of us can improve his basic skills.

PASSING

We begin with passing because it is the most basic element of a *team* sport. Passing has become more and more neglected and yet it can be truly a highly developed art. The ability to deliver the ball where you want it at the precise time you want it to get there is a very delicate, pretty, and important thing. And of all the individual skills it is passing that is closest to the essence of basketball as a team sport.

The idea is to get the ball to a teammate, the shooter, when and where he wants to shoot. Thus the pass receiver should have his hands in shooting position when he gets the ball, and it's a shame if he has to move his hands more than a few inches from ready shooting position to receive a pass and

For years Oscar Robertson was one of basketball's consummate players. His mastery of the basic skills of passing, dribbling and shooting made his game appear almost effortless.

then back again to shoot. The distance a pass is off target is thus doubled in terms of efficiency. Certainly there are exceptions to receiving the ball in the shooting position, such as moving the ball downcourt, and passes that begin a play, but the key thing is to be in the ready position when receiving the ball, ready to pass, dribble, or shoot.

Efficiency is the point. The best pass is the one that gets to its target most easily, most efficiently. That is why the basic passes are usually the best: the chest pass, the overhead pass, the flip pass, the bounce pass. Fancy passes, such as behind the back, are often counterproductive. They draw attention to the individual passer and break down the team concept. Any "great pass" probably has a great risk involved, but what we are looking for is a way to get the job done while cutting down the percentage of risk.

It's better not to throw a pass than to take a chance on one you don't feel good about or one that has small likelihood of completion. In the philosophy of passing, every bad or errant pass is the thrower's fault. Usually, a good pass is hardly noticed—except by the receiver who has been able to make efficient use of it. And he should acknowledge the teammate who has set him up.

Those of us who were fortunate enough to see Oscar Robertson in action have a perfect example of what we are talking about. He was unspectacular to the point that some people didn't appreciate his efficiency and economy of movement. With his dribbling and passing he could get the ball just where he wanted it at the right time, yet the general impression of the public was that his dominance as an offensive player was a matter of strength and scoring.

The Big O had the rare ability to utilize the talent around him, to get the most out of the natural abilities of others. He had complete visual command of the whole floor and complete physical command of his body and the ball. His dribbling was as effective as if he'd put the ball under his arm and walked to where he wanted to go. Similarly his passes were as if he went and placed the ball in a teammate's hands just where the receiver wanted it, with neither wasted motion nor useless flair. Lesser players seemed to have to do things the hard way or the fancy way.

Among contemporary players, there are a few known for their passing, such as Earvin (Magic) Johnson and Larry Bird. There are other players who are sometimes too flashy, but much of their success has to do with the surprise element. Even at the highest level of play in basketball today, an offensive star who makes a good, simple pass will often catch off guard a defender who is concentrating against a shot. Thus a Johnson or a Bird can efficiently use fundamental passes as potent offensive weapons, just as less heralded passers often do.

Dribbling is one of the game's most important skills. Here, head up and at full speed, Dennis Johnson drives to the basket.

Isiah Thomas, one of the game's better passers, has established good position on his defender in order to launch an accurate two-handed bounce pass down the middle.

Chest Pass

The chest pass is a two-hand pass, used when there is no obstacle between passer and receiver. It is therefore usually a perimeter pass, guard to guard or guard to forward. The ball is grasped in both hands, with spread fingers in a relaxed position. The ball is held at the chest and released with a flick of the wrists, directly to the target, with no arc, so that the receiver will catch it chest high. The palms of the passer will usually end up facing down, so that there is a slight backspin on the ball when released.

On the chest pass, the fingers are spread and the ball is released with a quick flick of the wrist, the palms ending up facing down.

Bounce Pass

There are two types of bounce passes: two-hand and one-hand. The two-hand bounce pass is used in the same conditions as the chest pass and is thrown in the same motion. But the bounce pass is more difficult for the receiver to catch than the chest pass and it takes longer to complete, so it should be discouraged in favor of the chest pass.

The one-hand bounce pass is used to get around an obstacle, a defender between the passer and the receiver. The arm is extended to the side and the ball is released to target with a flick of the wrist. It is helpful to use a crossover step at the same time in order to keep the body, or at least the leg and knee, between the opponent and the ball. It also adds extended lateral movement to get the ball around that obstacle. The ball should bounce about two thirds of the way between the passer and the receiver. It is not a V but a shallow skip bounce. The receiver should never have to catch a bounce pass above the waist but should get the ball between knee and waist coming into a ready position with his hands.

The bounce pass should come off the floor about two-thirds of the way between passer and receiver and reach the receiver between knee and waist height.

Overhead Pass

This is a two-hand pass thrown from hands extended fully overhead. The ball is held as in a chest pass, with both hands relaxed. Usually there is a fake down with the ball, then a quick extension of the arms overhead, and a quick release of the ball over the defender's head to a stationary target. This pass is very effective in feeding the ball into a player in the post position.

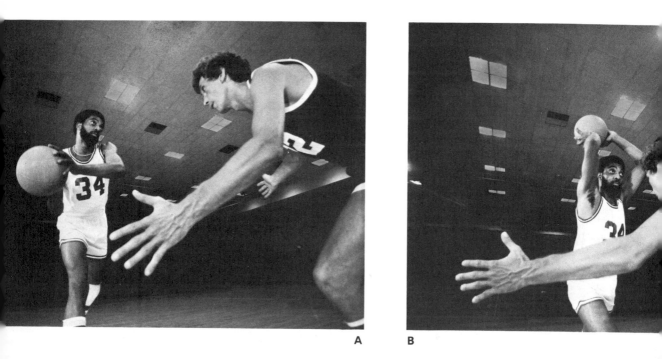

A   B

The overhead pass often begins with a fake down (A). Then the ball is quickly raised overhead (B) and released with a quick snap forward, palms facing down (C).

19

c

Flick Pass

This pass is thrown with one hand, either hand, by a flick of the wrist from a hand raised just above shoulder height. It should be a very quick motion, and it is used to get the ball through an obstacle to a target. There should be an element of surprise in the flick pass, so that it is usually set up by a fake, but the quickness of the motion is what prevents it from being a high-risk pass.

The flick pass is thrown from shoulder height with a quick snap of the wrist.

Baseball Pass

This is a pass used in the open court, especially off a rebound, for distance. It is important to use a motion like that of a baseball catcher—that is, instead of winding up with the ball taken behind the head, it should be flipped with a quick release from behind the ear. Palm and thumb should be face down at release. This motion will avoid a spin that would make a long pass curve away from or behind a receiver, who will probably be on the run and needs a straight ball to assure a high chance of completion.

The baseball, or outlet pass, is made with no windup. The ball is thrown with a quick snap of the arm, starting even with the head.

You should always have a target in mind when you throw a pass, not just a teammate but a definite part of his body. In most cases, your target will be the hand of the offensive player that is farther away from the pressure of the defense. Ideally every pass will be received in a ready position, so that the receiver may either shoot or pass or dribble as soon as he gets the ball. Most good shooters, especially when coming off a screen into shooting position, will already be in a shooting motion when they receive a pass, so the passer should put the ball in his hands just where he wants it.

Here, #32 throws a good, fundamental chest pass. Note the passer's relaxed hands, palms down, on the follow-through.

PASSING DRILLS

Half an hour of regimented drills every day over a summer will considerably improve the fundamental basketball skills. Here are three drills to improve passing skills. Remember that in an ordinary offense, try not to pass much more than twelve feet. The idea is to develop the ability to get the ball through a barrier (defender) to a target (receiver) about twelve feet away. Use, in these drills, whatever works—the flick pass with a quick movement of the wrists, the sweep bounce pass to get around a defender, the overhead pass to avoid interceptions—but without getting fancy with impractical, low-percentage, wasted-energy showboating. Find an efficient way to hit a target.

Lane-Pass Drill

For three people, use the lane-pass drill. A passer stands on each side of the twelve-foot foul lane with a defender in between. As the defender moves back and forth to cover the man with the ball, the passers should pass it back and forth twelve or fifteen times without interception. Rotate positions so that each of the three players is in the middle twice.

Running-Pass Drill

For two people or relays of two, use the running-pass drill. One player lines up at the inside foul lane, the other at the sideline. Running in a straight line the length of the court from baseline to baseline, the two should pass back and forth so that the ball never touches the floor. They should run in full stride, with no sidestepping, turning only the upper body while running straight ahead. Because they are running in stride, there is neither jumping nor dribbling. The pass should be chest high, the hands ready, the head turned with the upper body to be fully aware of the ball's location at all times. Ideally this drill should be accomplished as quickly as it takes to run the length of the floor without the ball, so that it would help to check the time with a stopwatch or to compete with other pairs.

The Strength-and-Reaction Drill

For one player alone, try a basic strength-and-reaction drill. Stand seven feet from a solid wall and see how quickly you can complete thirty passes to yourself. Constant measurement of this drill, repeated in a daily solitary practice session, will give you an accurate yardstick to check your developing strength with the passes and quickness of reaction to them.

DRIBBLING

Whereas passing has come into neglect in recent basketball history, dribbling has become overemphasized. Overdribbling is a common by-product of too much one-on-one play, and it is a difficult habit to break in organized team play, even at the highest level in the NBA.

Of course, every player should know how to dribble, should have command of the ball with the body. As Red Auerbach used to say with characteristic rough eloquence, the floor is flat and the ball is round; it will come back to you so you don't have to look for it.

The high dribble is used to get quickly from one point on the floor to another. The ball is pushed down hard out in front so that you can run as fast as you can while maintaining minimal control of the ball. The head should be up so that you have visual command of the floor. You should not have to watch the ball, so you can direct your vision in a wide peripheral range downfloor.

A high dribble is used when moving at full speed. Keep the ball well out in front and the head up.

The closer you get to congestion the closer the ball should be dribbled to the floor. Still the head should be up, the back straight. It is a simple fact that the less time the ball is out of your hand, the quicker it comes up, the more control you have, the less chance you have of losing the ball. Yet this fact is often neglected in actual play.

A good low dribble—back straight, head up, ball low and under control.

Fundamental to a sound game of basketball is the ability to dribble well with either hand and to change hands while shifting direction, never looking at the ball.

Although dribbling is a valuable basketball skill, it is probably the most abused of all the skills. Think of it as subtle flavoring to the essential taste of the game, like a little salt to heighten the pleasure of a good steak. If the lid comes off the container and you pour salt all over the steak, you'll ruin it. When one player dribbles excessively, four others usually just watch. Obviously, four players watching one pound the ball too much is contrary to any team concept.

Remember that in a set offense there are very few times you will dribble the ball more than twice. At most it is a matter of either bounce, bounce to a layup or bounce, bounce to an open spot for a pass or a shot. Otherwise it is a matter of moving from one point to another with the ball in order to make an entry into the offense, or in a fast break to get downcourt in a hurry. In both cases there is a premium on quickness, and since the ball moves in the air faster

than bouncing on the floor, the highest value is on dribbling *only until* you can give up the ball.

It is important therefore to know how to pass off the dribble in a smooth, fluid motion. The best way is to control the ball with two hands off the dribble and pass in the same motion. It may not look as fancy as scooping the ball with one hand and passing off the dribble, but it is safer, quicker, and more efficient. It also discourages the emphasis on one hand in dribbling. For dribbling to be an effective skill, it must be available for efficient use with either hand at either side of the body and without ever having to be watched.

For maximum efficiency, a player getting the ball should have the options of shooting, passing, and dribbling open to him. Too many times players surrender one of these options, making things much easier for the defense, by

Holding the ball low and trap dribbling off a rebound are dangerous moves. It is easy to lose control of the ball, and you risk being tied up. Instead, try to keep the ball above the shoulders.

what is known as the trap dribble. It is a trap because by blindly or thoughtlessly putting the ball on the floor as soon as you control it, you are trapping yourself, reducing your options, and making it easier for your opponents to defend against you. So, don't automatically put the ball on the floor when you get it. In the open court with your back to the basket, if you turn with a trap dribble, you risk an offensive charging foul or losing the ball to an alert defender —or you will have to pull up, having given up one of your options.

Even more foolish is the trap dribble off a rebound, especially on the offensive board. The rebounder has gone up, working hard to get the ball, and then risks giving it up by putting it down where anyone can grab it away or tie it up, turning in traffic where he might foul, and losing an option to avoid a three-second violation in the lane. The rebounded ball should not be brought down below the shoulders, and a dribble is the exact opposite of efficient play.

DRIBBLING DRILLS

Dribbling can easily be practiced alone. By setting up obstacles and dribbling around chairs; by working with both hands on the crossover, behind-the-back, and pivot moves; by bouncing the ball around and through spread legs in a figure-eight pattern—the mechanical skills of dribbling can be developed. Yet these skills should not be employed unnecessarily in game situations.

Other solitary drills can help condition the player to avoid bad dribbling habits. One is to exercise all the dribbling maneuvers in front of a mirror or a plate-glass window. By watching yourself in the reflecting surface you will learn to keep your head up, so that the unseen hand control of the ball comes naturally. Another is to practice catching the ball off the backboard, toss it about four feet away, and regain control in the ready position (for shot, pass, or dribble). This will help decondition the tendency to trap dribble.

The Dislodge Drill

For two players, the dislodge drill is excellent practice. Each player has a ball inside one of the jump circles on the court. The idea is for each player to maintain his own dribble while trying to dislodge the ball from the other player. To do this effectively and remain inside the circle it will be necessary to control the ball without watching it, protect it with the body while changing hands and crossing over, and still have the freedom of movement to attack the other player's ball and dislodge it or at least force interruption of his dribble.

The Full-Court Drill

This drill involves dribbling the ball five times up and down the whole length of the court. The first time is the high dribble in a sprint. Back straight, head up, you should be able to get up and down the court with the ball just about as fast as you could running without the ball. Use one hand going in one direction and the other hand coming back.

The second time you are anticipating pressure, so you dribble closer to the floor. You push hard from the endline to the foul line, stop in a crouch, back up, then explode to the ten-second line, stop, crouch, switch hands, advance to the foul line, stop, crouch, and advance to the baseline. Of course, you are maintaining your dribble throughout.

The third time is to practice the pivot. You dribble to an obstacle, imagined to be at the foul lines and the ten-second line, pivot, change hands, and continue in the same direction, having protected the ball with your body on the pivot. You plant your foot as close to the obstacle as you can safely get and pivot to turn your body between defender and ball, picking up your dribble with

A pass off the dribble should be done with one fluid motion, using two hands to bring the ball under control and for the release.

the opposite hand, so that you come out of the full turn from the pivot moving ahead in the same direction.

The fourth time is to practice the crossover dribble. You move obliquely upcourt, coming out from the baseline at a forty-five-degree angle. At the foul line you plant your outside foot with your outside hand dribbling the ball (foot and hand away from the defender), body low and head as always up, and explode in a crossover at a ninety-degree angle. In other words, if you are dribbling with your right hand, you plant your right foot, keeping your body mass low to the floor, and skip the ball across to a spot just in front of where your left toe will be; then you pick up the dribble with your left hand, having changed directions at a right angle.

Finally, the fifth time, you practice the crossover dribble behind the back; you shouldn't use this whenever possible to show off in a game, but you should know how to do it, to avoid the quick hands of a superior defender who could steal the ball by flicking it away from you on your dribble. The motion is the same as for the crossover—plant the outside foot, turn at right angles—except that you bounce the ball behind your back to the opposite hand.

SHOOTING

All movement in physical activities can be examined for efficiency, balance, rhythm, and grace, but especially those movements that require the highest degree of coordination. These are what could be called the "fine-art movements" in sports, and they include such tests of coordination as hitting a baseball, putting a golf ball, throwing a dart, and delivering a bowling ball. All are activities that require both great hand-eye coordination and the drilling of the body into a grooved motion by repetition. Efficiency, balance, rhythm, and grace all cohere in these movements as the body learns to do them the same right or best way each time. Shooting a basketball is precisely one of these fine-art movements.

The power for the shot originates from the floor, is exerted rhythmically, fluidly, up through the toes, feet, ankles, flexion of knees, hips, upper body, all the way through the arm, hand, and fingertips to the release. It should be a snakelike motion uncoiling from the feet on the floor through the release, a continuous, smooth action that in ideal conception extends all the way from the feet on the floor through the release from the hand to the path of the ball through the hoop. Up and in, it is all one.

The Set Shot

We like to start off with a youngster by having him hold the ball out in front of him in a natural position and drop it to the floor. He should let it bounce and catch it underneath in one hand, then throw it up in the air a few times, letting it settle comfortably in his hand. He should have it out in front of him now with his fingers relaxed, slightly spread but not overextended. The ball should be resting on the fingers but not touching the lower ridge of the palm. The weight should be from the junction of the fingers out to the fingertips, with the thumb spread naturally. Now he should turn the ball into shooting position.

The ball should be held just above eye level and off to one side of the head. (Remember that you aim a rifle by sighting along the barrel from one side, not from between the eyes.) The upper arm should be parallel to the floor, with the forearm straight up. There should be as much flexion in the wrist as possible. The classic shooters like Oscar Robertson, Jerry West, Phil Chenier, and Roger Phegley formed three sides of a precise square with the upper arm, the forearm, and the back of the shooting hand.

Now, with the body in balance, square to the basket with perhaps a slight turn toward the target, the elbow should point directly at the front of the rim.

The key to successful shooting is a fluid, single-motion delivery with thrust beginning in the legs, then moving through the body and arm as it is extended. The ball is released gently, not thrown.

Most great shooters will say that they aim for the hole (in fact, for the middle of the hole) but it is easier to talk and think about the target as just over the front of the rim. Visualize yourself standing in a phone booth; shoot the ball up and out of the top of the booth. The key phrase is *up and out.*

It is very important that the forearm be vertical to the floor because the elbow is a hinge joint, and hinge action should go directly at the target. If the elbow is out, the tendency is to drag it across the body. The shot is an extension of the arm, with the flexion of the elbow and a flip of the wrist. The two guide fingers (index and middle fingers) are the last to touch the ball as the elbow straightens and the wrist flips. With the ball in the air, wave good-bye to it—this is just a reminder that insures follow-through. If there is not quite a bit of backspin on the ball, you are not shooting or following through properly. The follow-through is simply the completion of the rhythmic fine-art movement.

On both the set and jump shots, the upper arm should be parallel to the floor, the forearm vertical, and the wrist fully flexed, all forming three sides of a square. The ball should rest lightly on the fingers.

As a set shot begins (left), the elbow should be pointing at the target with the ball slightly to one side and just above head level. The wrist flips forward at release (right) with the hand "waving good-by" to the ball.

36

Now, this detailed kind of analysis is probably not possible during the act of shooting. The analysis is too complicated. So try to concentrate on a few things: square up, point the elbow at the target, keep the ball above the eyes (otherwise you will be pushing, not shooting), and wave good-bye.

The Jump Shot

The jump shot should be no different from a set shot. Merely raise the platform from which the shot is launched with increased flexion of the knees and the jump. By platform we mean simply the level from which the shot is launched; the platform for a set shot is the floor, for a jump shot the level achieved by the jump. The platform should be adjustable; the farther the shot the more power you need, and so the higher the platform. Sometimes you need to raise the platform to get the shot off over taller defenders. The ball should be released at the precise instant that you establish the platform.

On the jump shot, jump straight up, releasing the ball up and out with the same motion as the set shot.

Byron Scott demonstrates the form that makes him one of the best jump shooters in the NBA. Note that he releases at the highest point of his jump, ultimately guiding the ball with the index and middle fingers. His eyes are glued to the target.

Think of yourself as in a cylinder. Jump straight up in the cylinder, establish the platform, and shoot the ball *up and out* with the same form as for the set shot. Your body should sway neither right nor left. You should neither lean forward nor fall back. The feet should return to the floor right where they left. You should finish the shot just as you started it, smoothly and on balance, ready to move either way to follow for a rebound or pick up your defensive assignment.

In many cases the target should be the backboard rather than the hole. With metal or plain wooden boards in playgrounds and driveways, this can be erratic. But glass or painted boards give a constant bounce and a steady target. It all depends on the angle. Once you are about fifteen degrees out from the baseline, the margin for error becomes more reasonable if you aim for a spot on the board rather than for the hole. That remains true up to about forty-five degrees or halfway on the arc from baseline to the top of the key. Some shooters, like Sam Jones during the Boston Celtics' championship years, are so comfortable with the board as target that they may extend the range of the arc. But the point is this: In general, if you are shooting the ball with good form, with the proper backspin, the rim will help you on direct shots from out front but not on angled shots from the side.

Free Throw

A foul shot should basically be the same as a set shot. Because it is a free shot —that is, unguarded and unhurried—a free throw should be a very-high-percentage shot. You should take advantage of the fact that you are free to do it as you wish. Take your time, relax, determine your own rhythm, and be as comfortable as you can. Remember that the longer you stand at the line without moving the more likely you are to get stiff or tense. That is why many players bounce the ball several times when they are at the line, and that is why it is a good idea to step away from the line between free throws—especially if you have missed the first.

Some coaches still try to teach the two-hand under-hand foul shot, but it is very rarely used anymore. Rick Barry, perhaps the greatest free-throw shooter in the history of basketball, used this shot, but there is only one other player now in the NBA who uses it. Much practice, endless repetition, and finding and keeping a groove can make any foul shot effective, but it seems to us unnecessary to teach a different shot from what players naturally use in most other shooting opportunities. So shoot free throws the way you shoot best, and do it often enough to make it a very-high-percentage shot.

Bouncing the ball a few times at the free-throw line helps loosen you up for a foul shot.

Layup

The layup or layin or snowbird should be as close to one-hundred percent as anything in sports. Traditionally it has been taught according to the classic form. From the right side pick up the final dribble off the left foot, take a final long stride toward the basket with the right leg, push up off the left foot, carry

On a layup, the shot is made off the opposite foot from the shooting hand. The ball is taken up as high as possible with both hands and laid softly off the board.

the ball up as close to the basket as possible with both hands, then lay it softly off the board with the fingers of the right hand. From the left side, turn it all around: Pick up the dribble off the right foot, stride with the left, push off with the right, and lay it in with the left hand off the board. Only coming right down the middle would you drop it over the rim without using the board. The whole point to this classic motion is to minimize the risk of missing the layup because of the forward speed of the shooter.

Nowadays coaches are less concerned about proper form for the layup. Players simply must get the ball in the hole. Go up with either hand off either

foot, use the board or not, but put the ball in the basket. A reverse layup—that is, driving through under the basket and laying the ball back up from the other side of the rim with either hand—should be as accurate as an ordinary layup, and it is useful to know how to protect the ball from a defender by putting the rim between him and the ball. It is also useful to be big enough or to jump well enough to come to a stop under the basket, push off with both feet, and put the ball down into the hole with both hands. All kinds of dunks have given even greater variety to the layup, but the basic principle remains the same—get it to the target the easiest, safest way you can.

To many players, the slam dunk, with its infinite and awe-inspiring variations, is the ultimate form of self-expression.

Hook Shot

The hook shot has been much neglected in recent years because with the domination of the passing game on offense very few players play with their backs to the basket anymore. But it is still a valuable weapon, particularly from the low post position, because it is a very difficult shot to defend against. A right-handed player receiving the ball at the left side of the lane is in good position for a hook shot. Holding the ball chest high with both hands, he should step laterally across the lane with his body between the ball and the defensive player, carry the ball up face high with both hands, extend his right arm with the ball in the right hand (his left arm now forming another line of defense), turning his shoulders toward the basket at release. The shot is thus more of a turn-in than a fadeaway shot. That puts the shooter in good rebound position if he misses. A right-hand hook from the right side of the lane takes the shooter

E   D

away from the basket toward a more difficult angle at the baseline. It is better from that position to take a turn-around jump shot.

THE THREE-POINT SHOT

In recent years, the three-point shot has had, perhaps, the biggest impact on basketball offense at every level—from high school to the pros. Now any team, no matter what its speed or size, has the chance to come from behind, and a team nursing a close lead can quickly demoralize its oppostion with one long, "downtown" shot. In addition, a missed three-point shot attempt often results in long rebounds, which can benefit the shooting team—especially the shooter if he follows his shot—and can thus keep smaller, outside shooting teams in a close contest. Too, no longer can defenses content themselves with sagging down

The hook shot begins with the back toward the basket (A) and a lateral step across the lane (B). The ball is taken up chest high with both hands (C), keeping the body between the ball and the defender. At release (D, E) the shoulders rotate toward the basket.

C B   A

under the basket; now they must go out and defend a wider area (in college and high school ball, the three-point circle is 19 feet 9 inches from the center of the basket to the outside of the line; in the NBA, 23 feet, 9 inches).

Teams these days generally incorporate the three-point shot in their offense in one of three ways: 1) as part of their transition game, where the three-point shooter on the run suddenly stops and pops, usually near the top of the key, 2) as a shot off a screen that directs the screened shooter behind the three-point line (more on screens later), and 3) as a shot after a pass from an outside man to an inside man, then back to the three-point shooter.

Fans love the three-point shot for the excitement it adds to the game; players and coaches generally like it as a powerful offensive weapon. A player doesn't have to be athletically-gifted or overly big to be a great three-point shooter; indeed, many of the best three-point shooters at all levels of basketball are neither especially quick nor strong nor tall. True, an effective three-point shooter must have enough strength to reach the basket consistently at long range; but, with practice, over time, and by developing your strength and shooting eye, you can start sinking three-pointers even in clutch situations. The trick is to *step into* the shot—most college and high school players shoot the three-pointer as a jump shot and find that stepping forward, toward the basket (but remaining behind the three-point line) gives them greater momentum and power going into their vertical leap. To practice the shot, start by taking jump shots close to the basket and gradually work back toward the three-point line, noting just how much power you need to propel the shot from each further distance. *Aim for consistency in your shooting motion, no matter the range,* and when shooting from behind the three-point circle, work on a smooth release and follow-through.

Every player on a team, no matter his position, should include three-point shooting as part of his regular routine. Who knows? You may be the one who has to fire up a game-winning three-pointer in the closing seconds of a game, and if you're a player who can sink the shot with consistency, your offensive worth to your team is 50 percent greater than that of the player who can only hit for two.

SHOOTING DRILLS

An attractive feature of basketball is that practice can be enjoyable, even for a player alone. Just shooting hoops by yourself can be fun, but you should keep several things in mind if you really want to develop your skill. (1) Work on shots that you will actually be able to use in a game. (2) Stay within your range;

never shoot from so far out as to require brute force to get the ball to the basket, or you will start picking up bad habits. (3) Keep track of your efficiency; that will give you a measure of your progress and consistency as well as providing reasonable goals. (4) If you are in a shooting slump, don't start asking people what's wrong—you'll discover that everyone thinks he's a coach. Instead, find a place where you can watch yourself, in a mirror or a plate-glass window, with or even without a ball. Give yourself a physical critique and you'll probably see where you have lost the natural motion, rhythm, and release.

"Beat The Ghost"

You can play a game with yourself called "Beat the Ghost." It's a ten-point game that demands accuracy if you are to win. You start at the free-throw line and you must make a free throw before trying any other shot. If you make a free throw, you score one point; if you miss, it's three for the "ghost." If you miss two free throws, you're down 0-6. After you've made a free throw you shoot from five spots on the court, baseline right fanning around to baseline left (always within range, so that the no. 3 spot needn't be way above the top of the key). You score a point for every basket you make, but it's two points for the ghost if you miss. Shooting alone this way, you may be shooting against your most difficult opponent.

Three-Player Shooting Drill

In this shooting drill for three players, use two balls. Station a rebounder under the basket and a passer at the free-throw line. The third player is the shooter. He shoots from the first of the five spots, either corner. He should come down on the spot and then move hard to the second spot. The passer feeds him the ball at the second spot, right on rhythm, so that he neither waits nor fakes nor dribbles but just puts up his shot, comes down on the spot, and moves to the next spot. Meanwhile the rebounder has given the first ball back to the passer for the third shot.

The idea is to pretend that you are coming open off a screen and must use the immediate opportunity to get off the shot. Shoot from each spot, then back around, ten shots in all. Then you rotate positions with passer and rebounder. Three complete rounds of this drill, thirty shots in all, make a good shooting drill for each practice session. But it is essential that you keep score. You are competing with your teammates and at the same time aspiring to your own individual standards.

Rebounding

Most coaches and commentators agree with the truism that the team that controls the boards wins the game. Rebounding, gaining possession of the ball on offense or defense when a shot is missed, is therefore both a vital statistic in box scores and a vital fundamental skill at every level of play. You've got to get the ball before you can do anything with it. That idea may be simple but mastering the techniques of rebounding requires hard work, particularly when those techniques are properly integrated in a team concept.

REBOUNDING: DEFENSE

It is not unreasonable to assume that a defensive player should capture a rebound. After all, if you are playing proper defense you are usually between your man and the backboard when the ball is released toward the target. Yet blocking out is one of the most difficult fundamentals to teach. Tall, talented players who can get the ball simply by outjumping others often neglect to learn how to block out—and pay for it when they move up in levels of play to compete with others who are equally tall and talented.

Here, the player from Marshall establishes position under the basket, ready for a defensive rebound while preventing his opponent from going for the offensive rebound.

To block an opponent successfully, work from a stable, wide stance, keeping your hips back and arms extended with elbows out. You can follow your man's moves by keeping one hand on his body.

Just a few times up and down the court, in most cases, will tell an experienced observer whether a team is well coached. Just look at two indicators: (1) Are the players communicating with each other? (2) Are they blocking out on rebounds?

According to former All-Pro Wes Unseld, an articulate master of defensive rebounding, there is a five-point program to success. (1) Think miss. (2) Make contact. (3) Establish path. (4) Capture ball. (5) Make outlet pass.

1. The first point is a matter of attitude. You simply have to determine in your mind that every shot is going to miss. It is an attitude that should be constant and a desire that should be consistent. Think miss.

2. Block out your opponent. This means physically making contact with him and then successfully keeping your body between him and the ball. You can't block out without finding the player you're blocking, and you can't focus your visual attention away from the ball. So you must make at least minimal contact to locate your assignment and keep between him and the basket. You either pivot on your inside foot with a cross-over step, or you pivot on your outside foot to swing your body around. Then you can move laterally in either direction to keep your opposing player away. The inside foot means the one closer to the basket or toward the direction of a target, but whether you turn inside or outside, you are trying to accomplish one thing—to keep your body between your opponent and that target.

3. Find the ball and move toward it. Remember that close to eighty percent of missed shots from one side of the basket rebound to the other side. Remember, too, that the average normal rebound travels slightly less than a third of the length of the shot. Play the percentages in looking for the ball, but when you find it, establish your path directly to it without giving an opponent an optional path. And this means that you must be as big as you can with your body when you go to the ball. Being as big as you can with your body means that arm position is more important than hand position. The hands should be in the ready position and held shoulder high, but that will be natural if your arms are in the proper position—extended with elbows out to give you coverage of a greater lateral area as well as to help your leap. Flexion of the knees is important in establishing the ready position for rebounding, and your extended arms will help you explode upward toward the ball. *Then* your elbows come in and you reach straight up.

4. The most important thing about a rebound is possession of the ball. If you can touch it with one hand, you can grab it with two hands with a little bit of extra effort. Capture the ball with both hands and keep it above your head.

5. Now when possession is certain, look for the outlet pass. The quick release can turn the defensive rebound into an offensive weapon, but inaccuracy can throw away the effort of getting the ball in the first place. And as always with passing, the higher the risk the worse the pass. Possession is primary; the outlet pass is gravy.

REBOUNDING: OFFENSE

Offensive rebounding is more a matter of philosophy and desire than of technique. But there are five points to remember, and they are valuable points, because nothing breaks the spirit of a defensive team more than keeping possession after missed shots.

1. As in defensive rebounding, an offensive rebounder should think miss every time a shot is released. The shooter is in the best position to rebound because he has command of the most information about where it's likely to go and has the best visual command of the flight of the ball.

But this seems contradictory because shooters should be confident and think basket when they release the ball. Nevertheless, awareness of form and

A good defensive rebound begins with an effective block (A). Maintain position when going for the ball (B), then bring it down with two hands and keep it above your head (C). Only when you have complete control should you go for the outlet pass (D), thrown with a quick, short release.

A   B

release—a mental image of what you're doing as you're doing it—can give the shooter reliable grounds for shifting instantly from the thought of taking a good opportunity to shoot to the thought of following the shot for a rebound. Perhaps this is why some of the greatest offensive rebounders, like Charles Oakley and Charles Barkley, are not great natural shooters. Early in their development they frequently missed shots, were conditioned to think miss, and learned to chase down the ball.

2. Avoid contact. It is in the interest of defensive rebounders, who Jerry Sloan says are basically lazy, to make contact for the purpose of blocking out. So don't help them. Fake; use quick feet to get around them, as if you are trying to get free for a pass; and follow the flight of the ball.

3. The most favorable spot for an offensive rebounder is directly under the basket, which is the worst place for a defensive rebounder. Pick a path to that position that avoids contact. Sometimes, the best way is to run out of bounds and back in under the basket.

C D

4. The offensive rebounder's job is easier than that of the defensive rebounder because the offensive rebounder doesn't have to capture the ball. He just needs to get a hand on it and keep it alive.

5. Yet if you can get one hand on it, a little extra effort can get you control with two hands. If you can capture the ball with two hands, go right back up with it. Don't bring it down where it can be taken away, and don't go to the floor with it. If no shot is available, then bring the ball back outside and start the offensive pattern over.

REBOUNDING DRILLS

Alone, you can practice rebounding by putting the ball up high on the board and going up to get it. You should develop habits of catching with two hands, landing in a wide stance, and keeping the ball above your chin. Always pretend that there are others going after the ball, and in that way you can practice good fundamentals of control, turning when you come down while protecting the ball, and faking the outlet pass.

Three-Player Drills

The best rebounding drill has three players involved. The simplest is to have a rebounder, a second player behind him, and a third as outlet. The rebounder throws the ball off the board to himself, while the second pressures him from behind. The rebounder catches the ball, turns to the outside, and hits the outlet man with a pass. The ball should not be brought down low; one dribble is permissible, but none is preferable. Next, go up for the ball, turn outside, and pass to the outlet man before coming down. Do each three times on both sides of the basket, then rotate positions with the other players.

"Three T's Drill"

This is probably the most effective drill for groups of three. The T's refer to touching, tipping, and tapping. The touching drill is done without a ball. Try to touch the net or rim. If you can't quite touch it, reach for it. The point is to explode to your potential each time you go up after the ball. Each of the three players leaps to touch the rim twenty-five times without pause, alternating hands with each jump. You should land on your toes, in the same position with respect to the baseline, with your feet spread at shoulder width. Quickness is called for here, so don't crouch in a sitting position. Come to a semicrouch flex position of hips, knees, and ankles, then explode back up and touch with the opposite hand. This drill develops the muscles used in jumping, and helps to avoid minor ankle injuries. If you're not tired after twenty-five touches, you're not exerting yourself enough to make the drill effective.

After all three players have done the touching drill, the ball is put in play for the tipping drill. The purpose is to develop fingertip control as well as good jumping rhythm. With complete elbow and arm extension, control the ball with the fingers, tipping it up and against the board ten times with the right hand,

When each player has completed the tip drill, all three in the group take part in the tap drill. Tapping calls for grabbing the ball with both hands and releasing it to a target in the same jumping motion. Player A tosses the ball off the board with both hands so that it goes over the rim about a foot and a half to player B's side. B explodes with his jump, controls the ball with both hands, and puts it back up for C, who has moved into A's place. A has moved inside and around behind B to take the next tap, while B moves outside and around C. In other words, the movement is a continual three-man weave. The circle keeps rotating while the ball is kept in the air for twenty-five throws. The drill practices the fundamentals of going up, controlling the ball, throwing it to a target, landing, and moving.

In going for an offensive rebound, try to slip around the defender without making contact and position yourself underneath the basket. Here Dennis Rodman #40, makes his move on the defender, #31.

Defense

Defense begins with proper stance, which is the common athletic ready position used by a receiver of service in tennis or table tennis, by a defensive back in football, and by a shortstop and most other fielders in baseball. The feet are spread wider than the shoulders and flat on the floor, weight is evenly distributed between toes and heels, and the knees are flexed.

The three basic principles of balance should be observed: The wider the base, the better the balance; the closer to the center of the base the center of the mass is (an inch to a half inch above the navel in a mature male), the better the balance; and the lower the center of the mass, the better the balance. Thus you should be flexed in a sitting-crouch position, back straight, and head up. Hand position is analogous with that of boxers (in the most primitive and natural form of offensive and defensive movement): Hands are open and spread shoulder width, ready to extend up, down, or out, to flick or reach, with equal opportunity.

Like effective offensive rebounding, good defense is a matter of desire. You have to want to play defense, and the motivation that comes from within is more important than technique. Several basic principles, however, can be mastered in the

Use two hands to grab the ball on a defensive rebound, and look for outlet passes to the side, or downcourt passes for the fast break. If closely defensed, draw the ball tightly to your chest, spread your elbows, pivot away from the defender, and dribble to open territory, or pass to an open teammate.

57

Desire, concentration and technique
made Dave Cowens one of the better
defensive players in the pro game.

development of sound defensive philosophy. At this point we are talking about
man-to-man defense, where the priorities of responsibility are first, man; second, ball; and third, area. Zone defense—in which the priorities of responsibility are first, ball; second, area; and third, man in area—will be discussed later,
as will matters of team defense. We are concerned in this section with one player
covering another.

Playing percentages on defense means making some logical assumptions.
Assume that the offense has some skill. A steal off a dribble is uncommon, so
don't make yourself vulnerable with the high-risk attempt. Assume that you
can't block most shots, so don't make yourself vulnerable to fakes and offensive
rebounds by going for the high-risk though spectacular play. Instead, maintain
your body position and stay on your feet rather than giving up your defensive
stance.

Much defense is a matter of self-discipline. Don't tell yourself to "stop"
your man; just make things difficult and uncomfortable for him. Make him beat
you with an alternative to what he wants to do and does well. Take his
preference away from him.

The guard covering the offensive guard with the ball has four assignments:
He should prevent easy dribbling, easy penetration, easy passing, and easy
shooting. When your man is dribbling the ball, let him establish a direction,

The woman from Carolina shows a perfect
defensive stance: feet spread wide with
knees flexed, back straight, head up, hands
open and at the ready.

and then keep him going in the same direction. Don't let him change direction, but force him whenever possible toward the sideline or the ten-second line.

If you are covering the guard away from the ball (off-side or weak-side guard), use a sloughing off or zone principle. The best way to identify this is by use of a pointing system. Establish your position by opening up with the leg closer to the ball, the inside foot back. Your shoulders should point to a position two thirds of the way between the ball and your defensive assignment. A string from the ball to the center of your body to your man's body should form an angle of ninety degrees. With knees flexed in the ready position, point at your man and the ball. Your arms should form a right angle; if they don't you're too close.

Remember that the farther you can play off a player and still dominate him, the better you are. And while it's good to help a teammate with his assignment, you must help yourself first to fulfill your responsibilities. They include preventing easy dribbling to the middle, controlling your man, and preventing easy backdoor passes into the area.

If you are covering the forward on the side of the ball (strong side), you have two primary assignments. One is to deny the ball to the forward where he wants it. Normally that would be in the area midway between the lane and the sideline at the foul line extended. You keep your inside arm up between the forward and the ball while your inside leg gives you body position under that arm.

Covering the guard (#32) away from the ball, #14 plays him loosely, using the so-called pointing system, with one arm pointing at the man and the other toward the ball, both arms forming a right angle.

Now, when he does get the ball, you must push off with that inside foot because your assignment is to deny the baseline. You want to force him to the center, where the traffic is heavier and where you're likely to get help.

If you're guarding the weak-side forward, you should use the ninety-degree, pointing principle of the off-side positions. Your responsibilities include preventing easy dribbling and preventing easy backdoor passes. But you have additional responsibilities. You must defend against the lob pass to the center if he is being fronted by your teammate. And most important, you must try to prevent your man from receiving the ball coming across into the low post. Force him toward the sideline or the time line, or front him if necessary (playing directly between him and the ball), but deny him the ball there where he really wants it, in the low post position where almost any forward is a very-high-percentage scorer.

A B   C

When defending against the center (here, #34), front him (A), staying between him and the ball if he's playing between the free-throw circle and the basket. If the center is between the free-throw line and the circle, cup him (B), putting the whole side of your body between him and the ball. When the center is beyond the free-throw line, play just behind him (C) and slightly toward the ball.

If your defensive assignment is the center (or any offensive player in a post position), your defense is determined by his position on the floor. If he's playing a low post (defined as the area from the dotted line at the front of the free-throw circle down to the basket), you should front him. In the intermediate area, from the dotted line to the free-throw line, you should cup him hard on the ball side. Cupping means putting a whole side of your body around your man between him and the ball, inside foot in front of him, inside arm extended around in front of him, inside hip right alongside. Cupping hard means playing very tight defense in this position. If your man is playing a high post, from the free-throw line on out, you can play a foot to a halfstep behind him and a foot or so toward the side the ball is on.

FOULING

Fouls are important and acknowledged parts of basketball, and aggressive defense will inevitably result in them. That is why each player is allowed a quota of personal fouls per game. From a coaching or training standpoint it is important to recognize that there are good fouls and bad fouls, smart fouls and stupid

#44 has suckered the defender into the air with a good fake and will have a clear jump shot, probably drawing a foul in the process. The defender should have kept his feet on the floor until #44 went for his shot.

fouls. At the end of a game, for example, a trailing team must often foul to get the ball back and stop the clock, even at the risk of giving up two points. Proper preparation will tell you which players on the other team are likely to miss free throws; they are the ones to foul, ideally by the players on your team with the least fouls.

In a game of balance like basketball it is the clumsy player who will foul more, the alert player less. But most coaches will suspect that players who never foul are not being aggressive enough on defense, on offense, or on the boards. A foul is sometimes unavoidable to prevent a sure basket, but if you are alert and quick enough you can sometimes prevent that sure basket with a foul *before* the shot that in many situations does not call for a free throw. Also it is sometimes useful to foul your opponent early in a game in order to intimidate him and assert a physical superiority.

Fouls are caused by being out of position, by not studying your opponents' habits so that you can anticipate their moves, or by not paying attention to coaches and scouting reports. But the most common cause of fouls is surprise. The antidotes, therefore, are attention, concentration, and preparation.

Here are several pointers that will help you avoid fouls. When your opponent is dribbling, never lunge at the ball, but go after it with quick flicks. Slap up at the ball, not down. Don't try to block shots all the time; keep your feet on the floor until your opponent is committed to a shot, and then it's good to go up with him and have a hand in his face. It is when you give up your defensive stance and balance that you are prone to foul. Remember that defense is played with the whole body, and if you keep your body in proper position your hands will take care of themselves and cut down on fouls. So will preplanning, knowing your opponent's strength, and overplaying to that side a half step in order to make him play to his weakness. Like so much else in basketball, fouling is at least as much a mental thing as a physical thing.

DEFENSIVE DRILL

The Line Drill

One defensive drill that is very effective for developing efficiency, stance, reaction, and footwork is the line drill. Two players face each other across the end line, the coach or a third player standing behind the designated defensive player. There is no ball used in this drill.

Because defense is played mainly with the legs—the legs have to get the defensive player to the right spot at the right time—the hands are taken away in this drill. The defensive player has to hold his hands behind his back. He gets in his defensive stance with his legs and body—but no hands. He watches the offensive man and concentrates.

On a signal from the coach, the offensive man moves. He can move in any direction along the line. He should use a lot of fakes and a variety of moves. He should use most of the fifty feet of the baseline if he can. Each player must stay on his own side of the line; that way they don't bump heads. The coach moves along behind the defensive player, talking to him, telling him to concentrate, not to go for the fake, to stick with his man.

It is the defensive player's responsibility to stay with his man without crossing his legs, to concentrate on the numbers (right on his chest), to stay in good wide balance, in good defensive stance low to the floor. The defensive player should be able to reach out and touch the offensive player any time he wants to, but he's at a disadvantage because his hands have been taken away from him. Since the average offensive possession of a basketball by a team is about eighteen seconds, this drill calls for a full concentrated effort for about fifteen seconds. Then the players switch position, and the reactions of the other player are tested and sharpened. Like the liberal prescription advice, this drill should be used as often as necessary.

Individual Components in Basketball

Basketball has now evolved to the point where it is possible to make some general distinctions among the five positions. While it is every coach's dream to have players who can, in the sports-caster's idiom, "do it all," it is much more likely on any level of play for a coach to recognize specific abilities and limitations in each individual of any group of players. We propose to describe here the characteristics associated with each position and the responsibilities of a player at each position.

One of the great things about basketball is that you can use the same training methods for a group of thirteen-year-olds as you do for the pros. Not only are individual superstars the models for the moves of schoolkids, but also the patterns of the game itself evolve and cohere and adapt from the highest level of organized play to the lowest. That's one of the factors in making it a universal game. And it's just a natural thing that in any group of players, whether it's an NBA franchise or a sixth-grade gym class, there will be one who is most adept at bringing the ball across the time line than any other: that's the player you want to handle the ball and initiate your offense. Any available pool of talent will produce discrepancies

65

Passer, rebounder, shooter extraordinaire,
Larry Bird epitomizes the well-rounded player.

in size, speed, and ability in the various skills; adaptation to position will follow from this general rule.

It should be kept in mind that specific roles and functions extend beyond five starters on most teams to several substitutes, so we will talk about the bench too. Other components, including coaches, managers, and officials, will be taken into account as well.

But it is especially important to remember that all of this breakdown into components, all of this analysis of pieces in the structure, is just a way of talking about parts of a whole. While we talk about fundamental skills, individual moves and responsibilities, transactions between two players or among three players, we are trying to approach a sense of the total game of basketball.

All of what is said in these separate sections only makes sense in the context of team play. Component moves are only parts of total patterns of movement. Without this understanding, what we say would be unnatural and misleading.

PLAYMAKING GUARD

Whether you call him point guard, lead guard, No. 1 guard, playmaker, or quarterback, he should be the best ball-handler on the team for the simple reason that he will be handling the ball more than anyone else. His physical skills could be generalized in the notion of thinking with the body. He should be able to have his body do whatever he wants it to do, regardless of size. Often, especially in early years of development, young players with playmaking ability are forced to play forward or even center because of size, but it is a shame not to allow ball-handling skills to develop fully.

The playmaker should be the extension of the coach, should think and react the way the coach would on the floor. The playmaker ought to be intelligent and quick; indeed, he usually is a good student and has the kinds of skills that make a shortstop on the baseball team or a quarterback in football. He should have wide range of vision baseline to baseline, the ability to take in the whole floor as he moves across the ten-second line with the ball.

In perceiving the whole offense, he must know the abilities of his team-mates at various spots and exercise judgment in using them. An offense is like a smorgasbord from which the playmaker picks and chooses, probing and experimenting, until he finds weaknesses in particular defenses and then takes advantage of them with the blessed offensive talent available to him. Five or six times up and down the court will tell the good playmaker what will work and what won't.

The playmaking guard is the quarterback of the team. He calls plays, directs traffic and generally controls the offensive flow. He has to be a top ball handler, as well.

SECOND GUARD

The other guard will usually be primarily a shooter or a defensive specialist. He has to be a good dribbler who can avoid double-teaming situations and is likely to be a better ball-handler than most forwards, but he is often a converted forward, bigger than the lead guard but not quite as handy with the ball. He and the small forward are sometimes interchangeable in roles—in other words, swing men.

The second guard should be someone who can play without the ball, carry out the options in the offensive patterns, and fulfill his assignments in setting up and using screens. He has to know how to get open because he is usually the last option in an organized offense coming off a screen or double screen to shoot from the corner. It is rare to find a big guard who is both a good penetrator *and* a good perimeter shooter. The preference would be for the latter skill, leaving the penetrating to others.

If the second guard has the defensive ability to shut down the opposing team's offensive threat at guard, the second guard may earn his starting assignment on the basis of that skill. But he must work to develop adequate performance in the roles required of him on offense as well.

SMALL FORWARD

The small or quick forward will likely be the most versatile player on the team. Ideally he will have as much finesse in open court as a guard, with much of the quickness, dribbling skill, and ball-handling ability of a guard, plus the physical stature to compete defensively and on the boards with the bigger players.

The small forward is usually the third man on the fast break, joining the guards to fill the lanes. The small forward should be a good outside shooter, but must also be able to go to the basket on a drive and to hit the offensive boards. Against pressure defenses he will often be used to break presses and bring the ball upcourt. Most offenses run a lot of plays to set up the player in this position for shots; often the first option is to go to him, so that he must move well without the ball.

On the other hand, the quick forward will be called upon to relieve pressure at the other end, adding strength to the defensive boards and usually covering the most versatile player on the other team. The small forward is thus pivotal in the transition game. In every sense, then, the small forward has to be a swing man.

A good small forward should be quick yet strong enough to go to the boards or drive to the basket. Adrian Dantley of the Detroit Pistons epitomizes the quality small forward.

BIG FORWARD

The big forward or strong forward or power forward is often the more agile of two starters who could play center. He should be able to utilize his height and strength, being as physical as he can on defense and in rebounding. He will probably not be as gifted with quickness, ball-handling, and footwork as a small forward or big guard, but the big forward makes his contributions in other ways.

On offense he should be able to shoot facing the basket or operate with his back to the basket. In other words, he should be effective posting up low or high or ranging out of the corners. He should be good setting or coming off screens, and he is a key rebounder at both ends.

CENTER

The center as a rule is the biggest, strongest player on the team. As such, his main functions should be as a screener, rebounder, and shot blocker. In other words, he should be an unselfish player who makes the other people around him better athletes. Ideally this would be true of all players, but it is an especially important quality for a center.

On offense he is generally the hub around which the spokes of the other players move. He has to be able to play with his back to the basket, handle the

Patrick Ewing, #33, demonstrates one of the center's prime defensive roles: blocking an offensive player from going for a rebound.

ball well, have good hands, and be a sharp passer. He should have a hook shot and should be able to turn for a ten- or fifteen-foot jump shot facing the basket.

Defensively he ought to be an intimidator, blocking shots, clogging the lane, helping out underneath against any driver. And of course he needs to use his size and skill to capture rebounds and initiate the offense with outlet passes.

THE BENCH

To a coach, the points produced by the bench, the production to be counted on from substitutes, the changes and adaptations to be made by use of the nonstarters, are like money in the bank. You don't want to spend all your savings on the first nice thing you see. And you don't win most ball games in the opening minutes of the first quarter. You win them later on down the line, and you need that reserve in the bank to be successful.

The ability to be consistent off the bench is a rare trait. Some players are "minute players"—the more they play and the warmer they get, the better they play. Substitutes have to concentrate very hard so that pregame warm-ups remain functional exercises instead of empty rituals for them. On the bench they need to keep their heads in the game so that when called upon they can perform with immediate awareness of the situation.

Substitutes have to be chameleons, ready to be transformed by a signal from spectators into participants. But they should expect and are expected to perform at the same level as starters. The dilemma is this: They should have the competitive drive to feel they should start, yet they should recognize their greater value coming off the bench, even when this implies an admission that others are better suited to start at their positions.

An ideal sixth man would have three distinct capabilities: He would be an instant offense, a scorer who can change the tempo of a game whenever he gets his hands on the ball; he would be an overpowering defensive player who can shut off the hot hand on the other team and thus break down the opponents' rhythm; and he would be an intimidating physical presence who can change the flow of a game by shifting the balance of power on the boards.

Obviously any one player who can do all these things would be a superstar starter, not a substitute. A team is fortunate if it has a sixth man who can do any one of these things consistently, and if it has special talents on the bench in several players to accomplish them all, it is blessed with excellent depth. The point is that substitutes should not merely be caretakers of the starters' positions, holding things together until the starters return to the floor. Substitutes should have positive functions and feel that they contribute in their own right to the team.

Adjustment, versatility, and compatibility are all key words in team concepts. Compatibility is significant here, and we're not talking about personalities in the locker room or on the bus. We're talking about having combinations of players who complement each other. In your backcourt contingent of three, for example, you want two playmakers and two shooters, with all three able to handle the ball. If A is a playmaker for B as a shooter, B may be a playmaker for C as a shooter, or C a playmaker for A as a shooter.

The same is true in the front court, where a rotation of, say, five players should have all the necessary complementary arrangements available. A player's function on the floor is always relative to who is on the floor with him. Thus, if a bigger front line is dictated by the game situation, a small forward should be able to switch to big guard. If quickness is called for, a big guard could move to small forward, a small forward to big forward, a big forward to center. That is why a team concept should embrace a bench that can provide advantageous alternatives, not just stopgap measures in a rigid, narrowly defined system.

MANAGER

At all organized levels of play up through college, the student manager provides valuable services to a team. His basic duties of seeing to such necessities as uniforms, ball, towels, and other equipment are perhaps the least significant measures of his value.

Usually a frustrated player himself, the manager will be first and foremost a fan. An intimate of the players, he will be in a position to provide a constant source of emotional support and encouragement to every individual on the team. And as an intimate associate of the coach, the manager will provide a useful liaison or channel of communication between coach and players.

Many coaches find that they become closer to their student managers than to the players themselves and often maintain such friendships through their lives. Many managers find that their jobs are good training grounds for coaching careers, and in any case there can be lasting rewards for those who contribute to a team in this capacity.

OFFICIALS

Basketball would not survive without referees, who have the most difficult job of all sports officials. But no one ever buys a ticket for a game to see a referee work. As administrators it is their function to keep the game going, under control, but to remain anonymous. An official who has worked a good game should not have impressed himself on the consciousness of player, coach, and fan.

The game is fast, the bodies often big and the players talented, and it is impossible for officials to call a perfect game. On the other hand, the referees have more of an effect on the outcome of a basketball game than in any other team sport. Therefore there are some basic expectations of players, coaches, and fans that officials should meet.

1. They must be decisive within a thorough understanding of the rules; every time a whistle blows it should be for a specific reason clearly indicated.
2. They must be consistent so that everyone knows what to expect from them.
3. They must never let a game get away from their control, or it could deteriorate into a chaotic melee, and players could get hurt.
4. And they must themselves be in good physical condition and sufficiently mentally alert to be in the right place at the right time to make a call.

The difficulty of meeting this last requirement at the pace at which the game is played today is what may eventually bring about widespread use of three officials instead of two.

Since it is impossible to satisfy every participant and observer in a game that requires as many judgment calls in officiating as basketball does, it is important for everyone involved to take certain considerations to heart. Officials should not think of coaches as their enemies: Officials should try to understand that coaches work hard with their teams day after day, naturally want them to do well, are prejudiced in their favor, and have little tolerance for judgments that hurt them. Coaches, like officials and other administrators, should remember that it is primarily a player's game, and no one but opposing players should take the final outcome of that game away from a team that deserves to win. And players, for their part, along with coaches and fans, should not habitually blame referees every time their teams lose.

The so-called home-court advantage in basketball is largely a matter of crowds influencing or intimidating officials. Although indirect, this factor can be a potent force when judgment is allowed to be swept up in momentum. Officials should acknowledge this, be aware of it, and resist it. Only sufficient training, conditioning, and experience can develop such discipline, and we join many other basketball people in hoping that more attention, effort, and expense be devoted in the future to the development of an adequate pool of competent officials.

COACH

Although the role of a coach varies from level to level of basketball, along with the relative degree to which it is a coach's game, some generalizations may be made. Every team, to a certain extent, will inevitably be an extension onto the court of the coach's philosophy of offense and defense, and in some ways will be an extension of the coach's philosophy of life. A true coach is a teacher; the practice floor is his classroom, the game his test. This is true at all levels of play, and it is also always true that tests examine students and teachers alike.

A coach wears many hats, and under each one there is a variety of functions. These may be grouped under three general categories: (1) organizer and preparer—the coach in practice; (2) field general—the coach in command of a game; and (3) legislator and enforcer—the coach as disciplinarian.

1. The coach in practice. It has been said so many times that it may sound like an empty cliché, but it remains true: Teams play the way they practice. If you want effort, spirit, and hustle in games, you had better get the proper attitudes in practice. If you want cohesion, intensity, cooperation, discipline, and efficiency in games, you had better have these qualities developed in practice.

If the coach acknowledges that he is a teacher, he should really approach his practice sessions with lesson plans. They should be orderly and organized, so that every minute is used with a specific purpose in mind. The organization of blocks of time should be followed closely, precisely by the minute, or else the lesson plan itself will be called in question.

The coach himself needs to be organized, not just day to day but over the long haul as well. It is a good idea to have a checklist of goals to be achieved over a complete season, arranged by the calendar. In that way the lesson plan for each practice session is not merely an arbitrary exercise but also a meaningful part of an overall master plan. And each practice, each game, each accomplishment can be measured against long-range ambitions.

In preparing a team for game situations it is important to make practice tougher than games will be. The coach has to subject players to stress, to put them at a disadvantage in every drill. Practice situations must be harder than anything expected in a game, because there is no way to simulate the tension or stress of actual play. But the coach can try, by keeping score of anything that can be counted, and by keeping time on anything that can be measured with a stopwatch. In fact he should, whenever possible, encourage competition and stimulate pride in the result.

In preparing for a particular game, the coach needs to focus on the special situations the team is likely to encounter. Use of time becomes a crucial organizational factor. The players should have confidence in a consistent structure of meetings, arrangements on the road, and in locker rooms and on the bench. And they should have a clear understanding of defensive alignments and the half dozen or so basic plays in the particular game plan.

2. The coach in command of a game. Success as a game coach, begins with preparation for a game. But that does not necessarily mean knowledge of the other team. Coaching should not be dependent on scouting reports. Knowledge of your own team is more important. Learn about yourself. If you know who you are, what your goals and limits and capabilities are, you should be able to perform at your best within those parameters.

One of the coach's most significant functions, then, is to scout his own team, on both offense and defense. The players should be able to make their own adjustments during a game if their coach has done a thorough job of preparing them. After eight or so minutes into a game, there should be no surprises. If the teams are fairly close in talent, there is a considerable psychological edge to be gained—a confidence factor—by letting the opposing team make adjustments on the basis of scouting reports.

The best game coaches are those who are most sensitive to the flow or rhythm of the particular game. There is no set of rules to learn to acquire this sensitivity. It seems a matter of instinct, a natural genius for the game; it can be sharpened with experience but it can sometimes also be dulled over a period of time as the game itself evolves and changes subtly.

But coaches can always keep their heads in the game by talking constantly to their players on offense and defense. (At one time there was a rule against this. The legendary Nat Holman got around the rule by learning to be a ventriloquist and throwing his voice so that his players got instructions from the stands.) You want your players, though, to be flexible, not simply to react by rote to commands. In scholastic basketball, game strategies are not overly complex. The college game is much more of a coach's game, because of the particular rules that apply and the relative sophistication of the players, while the professional coach operates on the subtlest level during a game—the option off the option off the option.

Problems common to coaches at all levels are substitutions and time-outs. Basically there are five considerations in substituting:

A. It is good to have a normal pattern of rotation by position, a standard procedure that gives a whole squad confidence in a routine.

B. There is often a need to change things instantly, as discussed earlier in the section on the bench.

C. Watch out for foul trouble. You want to avoid getting a third foul on a high school or college player in the first half, a fourth in the pros. Particularly important is knowing when to send players in foul trouble back in, knowing which players can play with foul trouble.

D. Defensive mistakes usually trigger the coach's hook. Usually a second defensive mistake will make a coach look closely at that player, and when the coach sees a third mistake he takes him out. Incidentally, it is a good idea to have a player coming out of a game sit down next to the coach. The point is to provide a framework for consistent behavior, to avoid a temper tantrum. You don't want fans to see a player's frustration. Let his mistakes be a learning experience for him. Don't let him sit alone with self-doubt, but when he's cooled down and understands what he's been doing wrong, send him back in with renewed confidence.

E. Watch for signs of fatigue. You have to know which players will be honest in signaling that they are excessively tired and need a breather. Others have egos too large to allow such signals, so you have to look for signs in performance. You can anticipate this by taking note of which players are working unusually hard, such as by guarding the opposition's best, most active player.

As far as time-outs are concerned, the coach has to find the right balance among physical reasons—when the team needs a break; psychological reasons —when the opponents' rhythm or momentum needs to be broken (or as Dean Smith takes pride in, forcing opponents to call the first time-out); and strategic reasons to set up a special play or to devise a way to break a particular defense.

3. The coach as disciplinarian. Many talented teams fail because of loss of discipline. The toughest opposition for them is themselves. But when we say discipline we do not mean regimentation. Teams shouldn't have to come out on the court and salute a coach.

Discipline probably begins with fear, the threat of being cut from a team or, later, of having playing minutes taken away. But the fear should evolve to a respect that, ideally, is mutual. Players respect the job the coach is doing; the coach respects the players' abilities.

Every society, every group, has its rules. Though a coach can't react the same to every player, the rules must be the same for all. You should never back yourself into a corner with rules, never have a rule you can't enforce. There must be one main voice in a team concept, and it is a lot better when that voice is the coach's. If it comes from a player, other players may be resentful and lose respect for the coach—and discipline erodes.

Basketball as a team sport involves several different types of discipline. The ability to interact and cooperate with teammates, the main concept of group-oriented sports, is one of them. That is the discipline of operating productively within the limitations imposed by and on a group. There is only one ball in play, but all five players have to live and function with it. The big ego, the type that produces surgeons and fighter pilots and golfers who have their own ball—sometimes with their own name on it—to hit the hell out of, is not suited to team sport. Only if the ego, through discipline, can be submerged into the group identity can special talents be employed. That is internal discipline.

The individual must submit to the rules of the game itself, to the rules of the coach regarding the functions of each position, and to the rules of behavior off court. These are matters of external discipline, and they may include such annoyances as curfews, proper nutrition, and the whims of a coach whose values are those of an older generation.

If athletics are an appropriate part of an educational program, and we believe they are, then a coach has a responsibility to educate. He can teach good eating and sleeping habits, manners of social behavior, and such practical things as how to pack a suitcase and check into and out of a hotel. He also has a practical interest in getting his players to stay eligible by keeping up with their classwork. In other words, a coach's discipline is showing responsibility to his charges by helping them to mature.

Basic Playmaking

Basic to every team sport, and certainly to basketball, is one-on-one play. All of the skills—passing, catching, shooting, dribbling, rebounding, even just running and cutting—must be performed by an individual, and he will usually be faced with an individual opponent at the time. It is therefore essential to have some one-on-one skills, but they must always be subordinated to a team concept. One of the most effective drills for one-on-one skills is as follows.

One-on-One Drill

The squad divides in pairs, one pair for each basket in the practice area. An offensive player stands at the top of the key. The other player begins with the ball at the dotted line marking the front of the free-throw circle. He initiates the action by passing the ball to the offensive player, then closes to a defensive position. The offensive player can shoot quickly over him, start a drive and pull up for a jump shot, or drive to the basket; but he cannot turn his back to the basket for slower maneuvers into shooting position. The defensive

On this pick play, #35 positions himself perfectly to block out—pick—the defensive man, effectively freeing #10 to drive to the basket or shoot.

player must protect against being susceptible to a drive, and he must box out on a rebound. He has to work to earn a shot, because the offensive player gets the ball back if he scores. The game continues for a limited time, just twenty seconds for advanced players, and whoever is ahead at the whistle rotates clockwise to the next basket.

ELEMENTS OF TWO AND THREE

If we keep in mind that two-man and three-man games make full sense only in the context of total team involvement, we can look with profit at some of the most elementary and indispensable plays in basketball.

A basic one-on-one move . . . a fake to the left, then a cut to the right, leaving the defender flatfooted.

Give-and-Go

It is hardly necessary to call the give-and-go movement a "play," so fundamental is it to basketball offense. And yet it remains as effective today as it has always been since the infancy of the game. One player passes the ball to another, breaks for the basket, gets a return pass as soon as he breaks open, and goes in for an easy shot. This movement is effective for a simple and obvious reason. When the player with the ball gives it up, his defensive man relaxes, however slightly and however briefly. It is human nature. That is precisely the moment to move to the basket.

The give-and-go move, in its simplicity, is really the essence of team play. By giving up the ball and then moving without it toward the basket, the passer sets himself up to be a receiver and has a better opportunity to score. And teamwork is developed by putting into practice these twin principles: (1) Give up the ball and you have a better chance to get open. (2) Get open and your teammate will get the ball back to you.

On the give-and-go, the offensive player on the right passes to his teammate (#42), then breaks free past his defender to receive the return pass and go in for the basket.

Pinch Post

A particular version of the give-and-go move is significant enough to be identified separately. It is a two-man play known as pinch post. The player with the ball, the giver in the give-and-go situation, waits until a teammate breaks open in a post position. Ideally this would be at the junction of the free-throw lane and the foul line extended. Just as soon as the post man flashes up to that open position, the passer gets the ball to him.

This pinch post play begins with #10 passing to his post man (A), faking (B), then pinching off his defender on his post while cutting around him to the basket (C, D). The post man turns and passes back to #10, now clear for a move to the basket (E, F).

A   B

D   E

The giver then becomes the goer. He fakes to one side and then cuts to the other side as tight as possible to the post man. Very likely this move will prevent the defensive player assigned to him from sticking with him. He will be screened by the post man as the cutter pinches in tight and rubs him off or picks him off against the post. The passer will then become the receiver as he gets free in the lane for a return pass from the post man.

85

C

F

Screen

Any time a player gets into position to shoot over a teammate who stands between him and any defensive man, you have the classic screen play. Obviously it is better to shoot when the body closest to you is standing still, blocking the defense, and shielding you from the world, than when he is moving, jumping around, sticking a hand in your face, and trying everything in the world to throw you off. Many basketball patterns are designed specifically to provide the advantageous situation of a screen or a pick.

The best screeners are big men who can effectively block out an area for a smaller teammate and keep his smaller defender off him. The big man usually has to be willing to sacrifice himself for team considerations, not only because defenders will be running into him but also because in setting a screen he will be reducing his own offensive potential for shooting or going to the basket. Most important, he has to set up in an advantageous angle or defenders will slide through or come around and force the shooter to go the opposite way from what he wants.

But it is a two-man play, and the other player must know how to make use of the screening body, however big and properly angled it is. It is a matter of judging both time and space to get open behind a screen, and players should learn to do it while dribbling the ball, after passing the ball (as in a pinch-post move), and on the weak side completely away from the ball.

A   B   C

Screen-and-Roll

The standard first option off a screen is the screen-and-roll play. From a position with his back to the basket, the screener can still see or sense when he has not successfully blocked the defense away from the would-be shooter. One of the two defenders, the player covering him or the one covering the shooter (or perhaps both), has gotten into good defensive position. He then pivots or rolls toward the basket, in the direction away from the good defensive position, because the defender cannot be in good defensive position against *both* offensive players. The screener then becomes a receiver, the shooter a passer, for a potential layup.

The screener pivots on the outside foot (in this case that means the foot away from the defensive pressure), crossing over with the inside foot, and turning open to the ball as he moves to the basket.

Incidentally, just as screens may be set up away from the ball, so may screen-and-roll action take place on the weak side. In their attempt to foil the screen away from the ball, the defenders may open a path to the basket for the screener, who is then free for any easy pass and score.

This screen and roll develops as #42 effectively screens the defender moving with #32 (A, B). As #42's defender shifts his attention to #32, #42 rolls free toward the basket and takes a quick bounce pass from his teammate (D, E).

D E

A B

#32's teammate is attempting to set a screen, but #22 makes the right defensive move by showing himself to the outside (A). This forces #32 wide, allowing his defender to stay with him (B).

TWO-MAN DEFENSE

The key to defense against all these two-man offensive plays is recognition. You have to recognize the play in time in order to defend against it successfully, so that you need to learn an alarm system. Any time your man moves away from the baseline, away from the basket, or away from the ball, you have to assume he's on his way to set a screen. The point is quick reaction to what is essentially an unnatural movement—away from, a direction opposite to, the instinctive inclinations of the game.

Once your man makes his move to set a screen, there are three things you must do with the object of avoiding a switch of defensive assignments (which usually provides a mismatch the offense can take advantage of):

1. Go with your man, staying loose enough to make contact.

2. Once he has set up in screening position, show yourself to the outside. About a third of your body (say, five or six inches) should be visible to the offensive man trying to use the screen, and you should have good vision of the ball and the cutter by looking past your screening man. The dribbler or cutter

will then establish his path to miss you. By making him veer, you will give your teammate a better chance to slide through, sticking with his own defensive assignment.

3. Communicate with your teammate. Warn him at least a yard before that he's headed for a screen that could pick him off. It is also your responsibility to call for the switch when it is necessary.

If you are the defensive man being screened, your first object is to get through that screen. If you can thrust a foot through, the rest of your body will follow. Now, if you can't get through and your teammate jumps out or slides over to pick up your man, your new assignment is to keep your body between the screener and the ball. He will probably roll toward the basket, but you stay between him and the ball, because you will be blocking the easy passing lane and you can expect weak-side help against a deep pass or a lob pass.

If you are guarding a player who passes and moves away from the ball to set a screen, you have to help your teammate in two ways. (1) Warn him about what's coming. (2) Give him room. Step back a yard so that he can slide through; never make it difficult for your teammate by forcing him to go around two men to fulfill his own assignment. The farther from the basket the screen is set, the easier it should be for the defender to step back and let his teammate on defense slide through.

Backdoor

One of the most common expressions in basketball, and one of the most frequently misused, is "backdoor." Basically a backdoor play is a three-man variation of the give-and-go move. It's just that a player other than the passer is the one who breaks open to the basket or the baseline when the ball comes into the post.

The backdoor often looks like a two-man instead of a three-man play. A player on the wing is being overplayed toward the post (toward the center of the court), and he goes the other way to the basket. But the play must always be initiated by someone else getting the ball to the post and inviting the overplay or the loss of attention. If the cutter is the passer himself, it's just a give-and-go play. Remember that the backdoor play takes place in a clear-out area, so that the third man in the play (the initiating passer) has the negative responsibility of not moving toward the cutter.

The primary function of the backdoor move is to clear an area impinging on the post man when he is handling the ball. By going backdoor you relieve pressure on the post, removing defensive congestion, and you serve as a safety

A B   C

This back door play begins to develop as #32 passes to his post man #34 as if to set a pinch post (A, B). As the defense shifts to counter this move, #44, the player on the wing, slips by #10 and goes back door (B, C), free to receive a pass and go in for the layup (D, E).

valve. Obviously, if the defensive pressure remains on the post, the player going backdoor is unmolested breaking open toward the basket.

The reason for the success of this move is not hard to find. It is the momentary loss or shift of concentration away from a player when the ball moves from another player into the post. When a pass comes into Bill Walton, for example, and the defense must be alert to possibilities of give-and-go, pinch post, splitting, and shots from the post, it is easy to neglect a player on the wing. But as soon as a defender turns his head from his assignment, that man will have gone backdoor for a layup.

Splitting

You come, I come; you go, I go. This is neither social commentary by Tarzan to Jane, or a modern paraphrase of Ruth's speech to Naomi in the Old Testament. It is the guiding principle of a basic three-man play in the context of a basketball team of five players. The splitting movement is a crisscross of two players cutting past the post.

D E

When the ball comes into the post, the passer is the one who triggers the splitting pattern. The questions are which of the other players completes the pattern, and how does he know. The answers are supplied in the preceding catchphrases. If the passer comes toward you to cut past the post man on your side, then you cut sharply across his back, passing the post man tightly on the other side.

If the passer goes away from you, cutting off the post on the other side, then splitting will be completed by a teammate coming from the other side of the passer. Your responsibility then is to move away from the play. The idea is to open up a lane for the second cutter, to balance the court, to relieve defensive pressure at the point of attack in the post, and to defend against quick-transition breakaways going the other way.

Let's run through that again. Say you are positioned on the wing, over toward the sideline near the free-throw line extended. Now, the point guard passes the ball into the high post. What do you do to carry out your responsibility in a splitting pattern? That depends on the initiating passer, the point guard. If he comes toward you to cut past the post man on your side of the court, you also become a cutter, crossing to the opposite side of the post. But if the point guard goes the other way, cutting past the post on the opposite side of the court, you move away to let a teammate from the other side of the court complete the splitting maneuver. You come, I come; you go, I go.

Double Screen

Suppose instead of cutting all the way past the post in a splitting pattern the passer stops alongside the big man. The second cutter may now have a double screen, two teammates to shield him from the hostile world of the defense, and he may have an easy shot as well. Not only is this a comfortable situation for a perimeter shooter, but it also sets up multiple options for one of the screeners to roll to the basket, perhaps by using the other screener himself as a way of rubbing off a defender.

Double screens may also be set up away from the ball. For example, a post man may break down from high post to low while the offside forward makes a move along the baseline to set up alongside him. Now, a guard coming around to get the ball can have a protected open shot on the baseline.

Stack

Two big men setting up low along the same side of the three-second lane are in a stack. They may set screens for each other or maneuver into a double-screen position either for the ball handler or for another player away from the ball. The stack is not a play, by any means, but a common deployment primarily used by a forward to get free on the inside by means of the center's screen. The three-man coordination is important here, as the passer must get the ball down low just at the time that the stack produced an opening.

Similar coordination is required whenever a double low-post pair or a high-post, low-post pair exchange positions with each other in order to create an opening or a screen. The third man, either by getting the ball inside or by moving himself into the pattern, is what makes these maneuvers productive.

Three-Man Defense

The keys to defending against these moves are the same as those listed above for man against man and for two-man plays: recognition, communication, determination, concentration. Keep your own assignment under control without making it difficult for your teammates to do their jobs. Concepts of team defense, which will be covered in the next section, are of course applicable here.

FIVE-MAN-TEAM CONCEPTS

Borrowing a term from boxing, we suggest that a ten-point-must system be applied to an offense in basketball. By this we mean that we want to see the following ten items included in any total offensive picture. We are talking primarily about playing against man-to-man defense, but many of the points are applicable in any case. And the list in no way implies priorities by number. All ten items should be present, whatever the order.

1. Fast break
2. Early offense
3. Total position involvement
4. Use of talent
5. Strong pivot play
6. Splitting
7. Screening
8. Two-man plays, pinch post, backdoor
9. Rebounding position
10. Defensive balance

Fast Break

The fast break is necessary because it is the easiest way to score, and no team that has to work hard for every basket is going to beat a team that gets easy baskets consistently. Those easy baskets are produced by proper use of numerical superiority, and you cannot afford to fail to take advantage whenever that superiority occurs.

Taking advantage means, first, recognizing that a possibility for advantage exists. If you can fill an available lane to produce a two-on-one or three-on-two situation you must do it, whether or not the ball is released to you on the outlet pass. Filling a lane *always* means an open lane, because clogging a lane makes it possible for outnumbered defenders to stop a break. So even if it costs you a couple of extra steps, you should move over to the next available open lane.

The three lanes are the middle lane and the two wings. Ideally, in the classic three-on-two break, the wings should be running straight down the court near the sidelines about a step or a yard ahead of the middle man, who has the ball. That means they will really have to hustle to get into the right position. At about the foul line extended they should break in toward the basket at about forty-five degree angles. The middle man will stop around the free-throw line and make his play.

On the fast break, the wings should run straight down the court, a few steps ahead of the middleman, then break toward the basket. The middleman pulls up near the free-throw line and initiates the play.

The idea is to force the defenders to commit themselves. The three-on-two break usually results in a short jumper rather than a layup, but if the defense covers both wings, the middle man should be ready to take the ball all the way to the hoop himself.

The fourth man, or trailer, should be about two steps behind and a step or two to one side of the middle man. The trailer must let the ball-handler know which side he's on, by simply calling out "right" or "left," and he'll be open for an easy jumper off a blind pass. The fifth man, usually the rebounder who has initiated the break with his outlet pass, should drag back for defensive purposes in case of a quick transition.

In the two-on-one break, again the idea is to make the defender commit himself so you can go the other way for a layup. Go to one side or the other so that you don't help your opponent by allowing him to stay in his best defensive position in the middle. Then the longer the defender waits to commit himself the more determined the ball-handler must be to go all the way to the basket himself. Three-on-one, incidentally, should give way to two-on-one; otherwise the defender will not have to commit but will block the middle, while an easy basket will often result back at the other end.

In any fast-break situation the player or players without the ball should follow through the complete path of their lanes so that the ball-handler knows

The key to a fast break is moving the ball up court before the defense can get back into position. Here UCLA's center throws an outlet pass on the run to #10, who is already well ahead of the defense.

A B   C

As this 2 on 1 fast break develops, #10 passes to #12 (A), forcing the defender, #34, to commit himself (B). #10 is then free to take a pass (C, D) and move in for the layup (E, F).

he can give up the ball for a layup or an easy jump shot. Remember that in the fast break the open short jump shot should be just as good a high-percentage shot as a layup. Remember too that numerical superiority means offensive rebounds are likely off a missed shot—another good reason for carrying the pattern all the way through—and that the pattern should almost always produce an open short shot if the defense should foil the layup opportunity. Now, if no shot should result from the break, the fifth man should move quickly into the play, and it is often he who will receive the pass that initiates the early offense, since he has the clearest picture of the whole offensive court.

Early Offense

If the fast break is not there, that doesn't mean that you should not hustle downcourt. Even when the numbers don't give you an extra player in the offensive zone, you may very well have the opportunity for easy baskets by moving the ball to an open man before the defense has a chance to set up. Again the key is recognition.

D E F

Whenever your team moves quickly to the attack you are likely to find a mismatch or a failure of defensive communication. The more pressure you put on the defense to hurry, the better your chances of developing a play before they have a chance to coordinate their defense. And just as with the fast break, the early offense produces not only open short jump shots and mismatches but also good offensive rebounding opportunities.

Total Position Involvement

There are five players on a basketball team, and all five have to be involved in the offense. There are always five players on the other team, too, so that if your offense doesn't make use of every position in your patterns and options, your opponents will be defending five against four or even three. You can't afford to give away numerical advantages. This may sound terribly elementary, but it is amazing how often in actual play a team with two or three outstanding offensive players will totally neglect the parts of their offense involving the other players, thus giving the opposition a defensive edge and allowing a cohesive team effort to defeat an opponent with superior talent.

Use of Talent

On the other hand, you have to make use of the talent available to you. It is a destructive practice for a basketball team to be so committed to a system that the players are forced into predetermined slots and roles. Every individual brings to the game his own unique combination of abilities and limitations, and the idea is to use the one and compensate for the other. Let each player contribute to the offense what he can, taking the shots he shoots best from the spots he shoots best from.

One-on-one play is often decried in basketball analyses, and rightly so in many cases. But there are times when one-on-one play is appropriate in a concept of total offense. For example, one-on-one play involves a whole team when, at a signal, four men clear a path on one side of the court for the fifth player to use his talent in a one-on-one match-up in the cleared area. When you have a Michael Jordan or a Dominique Wilkins on your team, it would be foolish not to use him in this way.

A one-on-one play can be run by setting up in a double stack low on both sides of the lane, with the soloist out front at the top of the key with the ball. The stacks can then clear toward the corners, peeling off one at a time, opening up the lane. If the ball is double-teamed, someone else will be open in good position at the low post or along the baseline.

With a stack on one side, two other players can be at wing and high post on the same side, clearing the whole opposite side of the court for the soloist. Again, if a second defender jumps out to double on the ball-handler, someone else will be open for an easy shot. And again, the one-on-one play is part of a total team concept.

String Pivot Play, Splitting, Screening, Two-Man Plays, Pinch Post, Backdoor

These and other two-man and three-man plays have been described above. The point here is that they are all basic and essential to an offensive concept. The team must be drilled in these fundamental plays and be capable of executing them whenever the opportunities arise. They have proven over the years to be sound and productive.

Moreover, even though only two or three players are involved directly in these specific plays, the other players must not stand around and watch them executed. All five must recognize the play, and each player must carry out an assignment. Away from the play itself, the responsibility may be to relieve pressure by clearing out an area, to move toward good rebounding position, to take defensive responsibility by guarding against a breakaway, or simply to balance the floor.

Rebounding Position and Defensive Balance

These two items go together in a complementary way. If offensive rebounding is overemphasized, and you have five men crashing the boards, you are going to get burned at the other end with easy baskets. If everyone concentrates on checking back on defense, you're never going to get an offensive rebound.

The idea is to have specific assignments based on the particular situation. No pattern should produce a shot without someone being in offensive rebounding position and someone else guarding against a breakaway. And then the idea is for each player to recognize what his assignment is in the situation at hand.

For example, suppose you have two guards splitting off the post. Now the strong-side forward is in the you-go-I-go situation, and where he should go is into the position of maintaining defensive balance. In fact, whenever a pattern calls for both guards to penetrate toward the basket, at least one of the front-line people must take over the role of safety.

ZONE DEFENSE

By the time you get to the college level, every team will have a zone press, a half-court trap zone, and maybe three standard zone defenses, as well as a man-to-man defense. Man-to-man defense is only as strong as the weakest defensive player on the floor, and zone defenses can hide man-to-man deficiencies. But there are other purposes and situations that dictate the use of a zone defense.

Pressing and trapping zones may be used for the purpose of surprise, or they may be used out of necessity. Standard zones may be used to protect a lead or to protect players in foul trouble. Most zones clog the middle, the direct lanes to the basket, so that they force offenses out to the perimeter, where the pressure is on them to beat you with outside shooting. Zones may be useful in compensating for weaknesses in size or strength on the boards. The best rebounders are kept close to the basket with the outlet men away; this will facilitate a fast break because your people are already in their lanes. Finally, zone defenses are helpful in changing the pace or tempo, and switching to and among zones should keep opponents off balance.

The simplest defensive zone to explain is the two-three. Divide the half

1-2-2 Zone   2-3 Zone

Zone defenses can take a variety of alignments, but these three are the most basic. Each requires specific areas of defensive responsibility.

court into five areas of responsibility. The free-throw line extended to the sidelines separates the two up players from the back line of three. Usually your two quickest players will play the up or chase positions, because each is responsible for a quarter of the half court from an imaginary center line to the sideline. Usually your three biggest players will form the back line, with the whole area divided into equal thirds, and with your best rebounder playing the foul lane.

The two-three arrangement, because it seems such a natural deployment by position, is a good way to disguise a zone. You may look like you're setting up in your man-to-man defense. On the other hand, you may set up in your two-to-three in order to disguise a match-up zone. Match-up zones are subtle variations of standard zones. Here an offensive man in your area becomes your primary assignment, rather than the ball or the area itself. You match up with a man in your area and stick with him *as long as he stays in your area.*

The one-two-two zone is also known as the "bottle" zone. The point man chases the ball all over the perimeter, while the other four, in a boxlike arrangement, shift in the direction of the ball. Thus, wherever the ball is, the neck of the bottle has turned toward it, and it will always retain its one-two-two shape. Its great virtue is that it should always be easy to get two men to the ball.

The one-three-one, often called the trapping zone, is very effective against post men—in fact, its primary objective is to prevent the offense from getting

1–3–1 Zone

the ball into the high post. One player is responsible for everything around the top of the key. Then three players are deployed close to the free-throw line extended. The two wings are responsible for everything up and down the sideline, the middle man for the high post. The fifth man roams the baseline from corner to corner.

The one-three-one is designed to trap the ball, to close in on the player with the ball by two defenders coming at right angles. If the offense sets up with the ball in the middle, the point man should attack the ball handler from the side, forcing the ball to the other side where a double-team set-up is waiting to spring the trap. The doubleteamers should not reach in for the ball but close at right angles, forming as big an obstacle to a release pass as possible, and using sidelines, lane lines, and the ten-second lines as additional barriers in the trap.

The one-three-one is a common arrangement for a zone press as well, though variations of two-two-one and one-two-one-one ("diamond and one") are also popular. Any of these are used primarily to speed up tempo. By trying to double-team the ball anywhere on the floor, the defense is virtually forcing the offense to look for the long pass and quick opening to the basket, gambling on a turnover at the risk of a quick basket, but at worst getting the ball back very quickly in a game that has had the throttle opened wide.

ZONE OFFENSE

Every team must come equipped with a zone offense to attack every zone defense. Good outside shooting is always effective, but is rarely reliable over the long run. In fact, many of the tactics and techniques described above in man-for-man offenses may be equally successful against zones. Although it is a good idea to move the ball quickly against a zone—remember that the priorities of defensive responsibility in zone defenses are (1) ball, (2) area, and (3) man in area—to wear it down, because the ball can be passed much more quickly than the men in the zone can move, it is also a good idea to have player movement. If you just stand around the perimeter passing the ball, you're helping the defense adjust to a stationary offense.

Now, having established the importance of player movement, we can see the value of specific movements. For instance, when a ball-handler can penetrate the front line of a zone defense, he is at least as troublesome as in man-to-man penetration. Now the defense has to adjust by leaving a whole *area* exposed and vulnerable instead of just one player.

It is also effective to split the seam of a zone with passes, just as passing offenses in football do. If you can move to a position where defensive responsibility is ambiguous you can upset the zone, either by being open yourself or by creating an opening elsewhere for a teammate. Thus the pass that splits the seam in a zone forces the defense to commit strength to a border area and underdefend another area.

If this sounds like a recommendation to use post play against a zone, that is quite accurate. The pass into the post is in fact a splitting of seams against any defense, and post plays work well against virtually any zone, just as standard screen plays do.

The strength of most zone defenses is inside, and the best way to defeat (as well as demoralize) them is to attack them inside. Where only the third defensive responsibility is a man in the area, the offense should take advantage of such priorities in defensive thinking by pressuring the areas close to the basket with players penetrating, cutting through, and screening. Even if the ball cannot consistently be brought inside, penetrators are often in advantageous positions for offensive rebounding off outside shots.

It is harder to block out on rebounds from a zone defense because it is hard to define or identify individual rebounding responsibilities. Thus there will be lanes open to the rebounds, and a zone offense should take advantage of this by hitting the offensive boards.

In general, the particular deployment of the zone defense should dictate the way your zone offense can most effectively attack it. Look for the seams and attack them by occupying as many men on the perimeter of their zoned areas as possible.

Specifically, against the two-three, you should attack the middle, its weak point. Once you're past the front line of defense you are often two against one in the lane. The one-two-two is weak against a high post man, so that is where you go after it. Come down the side, rather than the middle, opening a wide angle for a pass toward the center, where your high post man will flash into an open area. Your cutters may then break open behind the ball toward the basket.

The most vulnerable area in the one-three-one is the corner on either side, so you should go after it on one side or the other. Try to occupy two defenders at the perimeter of their areas and then attack from behind the ball by overloading the other areas. Think of your pattern as a grid (and this applies to other zones as well). If you can visualize a one-three-one deployment of the defense on the court, superimpose an arrangement that will counter it. It will look like an off-center two-one-two (against a two-three, your superimposition will look like a compressed three-two).

TRANSITION GAME

In a sense, the transition game in basketball is like the play of special teams in pro football. It has been very little emphasized until recent years, and yet a large number of games are decided by transitional play or the efforts of special teams.

The area between the foul lines on a basketball court is a no-man's-land, and what takes place in this area is basically dull to player and spectator alike. That is precisely why the transition game is neglected, because that is precisely where it is primarily played.

Whether we are talking about conversion from offense to defense or from defense to offense, we have to talk about quickness of recognition and quickness of reaction. By the time the transition has been completed—that is, by the time the ball comes back across the time line—it is usually too late to make a proper adjustment and you have lost the transition game.

The time line, therefore, should serve as a constant reminder. On transition to offense you should have picked up, by the time you hit that line at midcourt, the possible openings for a break or an advantage or an early offense. You should have recognized the available lane, the desired position as trailer, the open spot for a high-percentage shot, or the opportunity for a mismatch.

On transition to defense, by the time you hit that line at midcourt, you should have picked up your defensive assignment. Often you will have had to make an instant adjustment to a potential fast-break situation and have picked up a player other than your regular assignment. Teams that get beat on the fast break sometimes fail to get back on defense at all, but more often they fail to adjust by picking up the lanes and especially by forcing the ball (the lead man with the ball) out of his ideal route as soon as possible. They can't run a fast break against you if you pick up the ball at the time line.

Defending two against three is a coordinated tandem effort. The closest man should pick up the man with the ball and force him out of the classic pattern. The other defender will go with the first pass, and then they should alternate from that point on, taking turns going with the next man who receives the pass.

THE SHOT CLOCK

There's no doubt that the 45-second shot clock (in the pros it's a 24-second clock; in the women's college game, 30 seconds) has had a big impact on both team offenses *and* defenses at the collegiate level. No longer can college teams who have the lead go into game-closing stalls, and the clock has forced college coaches to develop offenses that attack the basket more quickly and succinctly, with finer-tuned plays involving a minimum number of passes. True, college offenses can still play a control game; even the NBA with its 24-second clock, has teams like the Detroit Pistons and the Utah Jazz, who are proficient, when to their advantage, at melting the clock before every shot.

Still, the clock has sped up the college and pro game for the good, and ensured an intense level of play down to the last second. In addition, college and pro coaches have found it easier to sell their teams on the idea of concentrating on defense, since all that's required of players is 45 (or 30, or 24) seconds of concentration at a clip. If basketball is to go through any more rule changes in the future, it might consider standardizing the shot clock to 30 seconds worldwide, giving the pros a bit more time to set up offensive plays, while giving men's teams at the college level (and, perhaps, one day, at the boys' and girls' high school level as well) a bit less opportunity to control a game's tempo.

TEAM DEFENSE

Like everything else that is good about basketball, defense is properly a coordinated team effort. Everything we have said about defense for one or two or three players must be taken in the context of a team of five. And most of our generalizations here apply to both zone and man-to-man defenses.

Establish defense in a cone from the center of the basket out. There is little point in setting up most defenses farther out than about a yard beyond the top of the key. Make opponents beat you, if they can, from outside your cone of defense. Keep offensive players and the ball out on the perimeter of that cone. The closer they get to the basket, the more congested the defense must be, the tougher you must make it for them to penetrate into your area of high vulnerability. There is also little point to a harassing man-to-man "war" defense away from the ball, because you give up nothing by allowing a pass from player to player or any movement parallel to the baseline.

The terrain of a basketball court offers some natural assistance for the defense to make use of. The time line, once crossed by the offense, gives you a wall to push them against with pressure or halfcourt-trapping defenses. The sidelines also offer natural boundaries to inhibit the offense. Even the baseline can be used to the advantage of the defense, since it extends behind the basket. The basic principle is to deny a big man the baseline, while for the little man on offense the baseline does little good. Finally there is the foul lane, where the defense has things two ways: Denying the offense the ball in your most vulnerable area is required for only three seconds at a time, while on the other hand if you can keep an offensive player in the lane for three seconds you may be awarded the ball on a violation.

Whether your defensive priorities are (1) man, (2) ball, and (3) area, or (1) ball, (2) area, and (3) man in area (man-to-man or zone), or perhaps some combination of the two, your concentration on fulfilling your own responsibilities will always help your teammates to carry out their assignments. Helping out is fine as part of a team effort, but you will have to worry less about helping out when every player is helping the team by playing his own defensive role.

Finally, there is the matter of tempo. It is generally assumed that the offense will dictate the tempo of a game, but that is not always the case. By forcing an offense out of the patterns it wants to run, the defense can have a great deal to say about pace. This is true even in the most extreme cases of slowdown, delay, spread, stall, and four-corner offenses (which even college and pro teams attempt within the limit of the shot clock). By overplaying the ball and forcing or funneling such offenses down toward the basket, you can restore a faster tempo even if you have to trade baskets for a while to do it.

Basketball for the Spectator

One of the most effective training and learning devices for a sport is intelligent watching of how it is played. But most viewers get too caught up in the drama or results of a game to benefit much from observation. This chapter is designed to help you know what to look for when you are watching a game. It could help you be a better player as well as enrich your experience as a spectator.

Entirely too much has been made, recently, about deception as the essential, distinctive element in basketball. All major team sports use deception. Football, for example, has misdirection plays, play-action passes, disguised zones and blitzes, and countless other strategies intended to deceive.

Baseball has the basic confrontation of pitcher trying to deceive batter, with subordinate strategies of base running, pickoff plays and disguised defenses, all designed to deceive, not to mention the covert codes and signals of managers, coaches, battery, and infielders all engaged in rituals of secrecy and counterespionage. Even the straightforward game of ice hockey, with its cold code of intimidation, has its own jargon for tricky moves. The word "deke"—from "decoy"—ultimately derives from the same root as "deception."

Basketball is a physical game, and one of the pleasures of watching it is following the intense matchups that develop between offense and defense.

Basketball has now, by a measure of combined participation and "spectation," become America's national pastime. And it is not by virtue of its reliance on deception that it has achieved this eminence. Backboards and hoops are not the universal decorations of playgrounds and driveways—urban, suburban, and rural—just so a whole population can practice to deceive. Rather, the phenomenon is testimony to the complex of beauties and skills, of physical and mental coordination, that constitute the essence of the game.

Basketball, as a fan's eyewitness delight, brings people out to games, more and more, at every level. It has inspired the kind of involvement that sometimes makes a fan cry out the single word "basketball," drawing it out in a litany of varied expressiveness—in praise of a great play, in despair at irrelevant action, in the joy of the whole experience. It is in the spirit of this chant of "basketball" that the following suggestions are offered for basketball watching at all levels of play.

First, try not to focus sharply just on the ball (a recommendation to officials as well as to fans and even to coaches). Try to let your "eyes go soft," as George Leonard says in *The Ultimate Athlete*, so that you can take in the arrangement and movement and rhythm of all ten players, but especially as the two groups of five are deployed. Then look for some of the traditional patterns.

The fast break. To see this pattern well, you must take in the full court. As soon as a defensive rebound appears likely, look for the positions taken by the guards for outlet passes. Then watch the opportunities for numerical advantages. Three-on-two or two-on-one are the ideal situations.

You may notice how often fast-breaking high school teams will simply use their speed to get downcourt for the first available shot, sometimes with the rebounder bringing the ball down himself. College teams will usually fast break from a short outlet pass, creating excitement by advancing in a crowded rush rather than clearing the break downcourt to the simplest advantage.

The operative phrase is "filling the lanes." Against one defender the idea is to have two players attacking in tandem, producing a layup from one side when the defender has committed himself to the other. You may notice how even good college teams will pursue a three-on-one advantage, which actually helps the defender to keep the middle shut off while forcing more difficult angles on the outside lanes. One breaker should pull up, yielding to two-on-one. Besides, three-on-one will often produce a quick basket in response at the other end. In a three-on-two situation, the classic fast break, as the pros play it, has the ball in the middle until the defensive commitment is made. In this attack the short open jump shot is as good a percentage shot as the driving layup.

Most important, in watching the fast break, look for the trailer, the fourth man coming downcourt to take up an open position over the shoulder and just to the side of the man in the middle. In exceptional cases the rebounder will become the second trailer, filling the fifth lane to the last open spot.

Continuity. Once a team has set up on offense—that is, when all five players have been deployed in their customary positions—look for patterns of movement. How many people are stationary? If one or two, these "posts" should be the hubs of the attack, while the others will be moving around them, exchanging positions with each other, trying to create an open shot from a selected area. If all five are moving, constantly shifting position, try to see the method involved. It will probably be either a weave or a shuffle, designed to free someone for a change-of-direction cut to the basket. The weave is basically a circular movement, the shuffle a regular exchange of places in paths parallel to the foul lane. The key here is to watch a ball-handler after he gives up the ball. Instead of keeping your eye on the ball, as all athletes are taught to do, follow the passer as he moves through the whole pattern.

The basic plays in basketball, familiar to most fans, involve only two players (give and go, screen, screen and roll) or three (backdoor, double screen). Now when you see one of these, try to see what the other two or three players are doing. Are they standing still and watching? Are they moving into position for the transition to defense? Are they offering an offensive alternative? Are they positioning for an offensive rebound or an optional pass? The answers to these questions will tell you not only how the team is playing, but also how well it is playing. The keys to look for here are the ways a team balances the floor and sets screens on the weak side—that is, how they play away from the ball.

Zone defense. Stationary zones are as old as basketball (ninety years old in December 1981), but when zones began to shift and slide and move (around 1930), the whole game was revolutionized. The advantages of these defenses are many: preventing the opposition from dictating your positioning on the floor, controlling the tempo of the game, keeping your rebounders under the basket, clogging the middle, putting pressure on the ball, allowing for smooth transition to offense (especially on a fast break), and protecting against foul trouble.

The simpler zones—three-two, two-three, and one-two-two—are those most commonly used by high schools. Remember that the basic deployment of a zone defense will not be revealed until the offense attacks it. Too early identification is misleading because coaches want to disguise zones. The spectator's key to recognition is the same as the offense's: Watch a guard, after he passes the ball off, run through the defense and see how the zone deploys against him.

Occasionally a dominant, mobile big man will play the middle of a two-one-two. Now, if the two men out front are given individuals to guard, you have a triangle-two. Like the box-and-one defense, this is supposed to retain some zone advantages while defending an outstanding shooter or two. One of the most effective zones, often seen on the college level, is the one-three-one trap zone, developed by the innovative Clair Bee at Long Island University and honed by Tennessee's tenacious Ray Mears.

Perhaps best of all is the disguised zone, a match-up arrangement in which quick players find personal assignments within designated areas—pressuring the ball, cutting off passing lanes, and preventing the open shot from the weak side. Not long ago, a well-drilled college team played this zone so effectively against a superior team that a prominent coach never realized his team had beaten a zone defense.

It is very interesting to watch the pros play zone defense, which is technically against the rules in the NBA. They call it "team defense" and "helping out on D," and it works like this: The big man, the center, blocks the lane; guards allow their man to penetrate; forwards drop off to help out, while forcing their men toward the baseline.

All this improves rebounding percentages and releases guards for breakaway possibilities; and it must be done fairly subtly to avoid officials' whistles. When you see a zone defense, look for the offense to move the ball more and their players less, arranging their five in a pattern that offsets the defense, such as two-one-two against a one-three-one. Again, let your eyes go soft; take in the whole scene. And again the key to discerning the pattern is to look away from the ball.

All this is not to deny the importance of the one-on-one aspect of basketball, in which the basic athletic skills—running, jumping, throwing to a target—are required in a way that balances size, strength, and speed with coordination, cleverness, quickness, and timing. But this elemental singleness is rendered intricately complex and aesthetically satisfying when the individuals are placed in a five-versus-five context. However familiar the basic patterns are, the possibilities for variation are infinite.

The cerebral dimension of basketball, where mental processes of recognition and response, invention and analysis, acknowledgment and analogy must be as strong and quick and complete as the physical, contributes greatly to the enjoyment of both player and spectator. Where the strategies of baseball are themselves part of the ritual function of the game and are more like slow-motion checkers than championship chess, and those of football are like projecting tic-tac-toe to the level of war-game spectacles, the thinking parts of basketball, in actual play, are like combining the lightning attack and response of an *épée* duel with finding the optional solutions to a sequence of variable algebraic-geometric problems.

Scouting reports and statistical studies in basketball do not determine precise courses of action as they do in baseball, but they do suggest probabilities for success in determining a style or tempo or general plan of play. Unlike football, a basketball play is a pattern with multiple variations, with each variation having a number of options measurable only by the number of moves each player can make, times the moves of his teammates, times the possible defensive adjustments.

But the intellectual element is inseparable from the physical in basketball, the smarts from the moves. Indeed, the beauty of the sport lies in its integration of all the elements of athletic appeal, including psychological, emotional, aesthetic, and philosophical. It is this charged tensiveness that makes basketball the most beautiful and the most exhilarating of our major sports, and only by seeing it whole can the fan appreciate it fully.